HOW TO GROW ROSES

HOW TO GROW ROSES

A COMPREHENSIVE ILLUSTRATED DIRECTORY OF TYPES AND TECHNIQUES

South Dublin Libraries
www.southdublinlibraries.ie

ANDREW MIKOLAJSKI

CONSULTANT: LIN HAWTHORNE

LORENZ BOOKS

Contents

Introduction

Highly prized for centuries, the rose is justly called the Queen of Flowers. It is probably true to say that for as long as people have made gardens, they have grown roses in them. Indeed, it would be impossible to exaggerate the rose's importance as the *nonpareil* among garden plants, and its mystique transcends the usual cultural barriers. The rose is the quintessential flower of summer, and with its myriad hues, scents and shapes, it is the perfect companion to many plants in the garden. Once established, the rose will continue to give pleasure for many years.

■ RIGHT
'Queen Mother' is a dwarf cluster-flowered rose with glossy leaves and pink blooms. It has a spreading habit or can be used in a container.

Introduction

The long history of rose breeding means that today we enjoy an enormous variety of lovely plants. Apart from the beauty of the flowers, many modern varieties have a long flowering season and good disease resistance. There are forms and styles suitable for nearly every situation, from diminutive patio bushes to huge ramblers cascading from pergolas. The range of colours has never been wider, either, from delicate pastels to vibrant reds, yellows and oranges.

■ LEFT
The award-winning 'Top Marks', with its radiant orange-red flowers, is a classic example of a dwarf cluster-flowered or patio rose.

■ BELOW
One of the best of the yellow roses, the cluster-flowered (floribunda) 'Arthur Bell' shines out against a backdrop of clipped yew.

We have come to expect a great deal from roses, and with thoughtful choice and careful cultivation they reward us with glorious flowers from spring until the dark days of winter; with scent that fills the summer garden and lingers on in oils, preserves and pot-pourri; and with decorative hips, leaves and even thorns.

The genus *Rosa* actually includes some 150 species of evergreen and deciduous shrubs and climbers as well as many

■ RIGHT
'White Pet', one of the first miniature roses, has stood the test of time.

thousands of hybrid cultivars, which have been developed from the species over the centuries. The rose has been known in cultivation since humankind first gardened, so we should not be surprised that there are roses to suit almost every climate and situation.

Roses occur naturally in a wide range of habitats. In the wild, the majority of roses bloom only once, usually in one glorious and frequently spectacular summer flush, followed by the hips or fruits that guarantee the next generation. Over the centuries, however, rose breeders have succeeded in creating not only plants that produce more and better flowers but also many willing, hard-working shrubs that display their flowers repeatedly or continuously over very many months – a feature that cannot be equalled by any other single group of shrubs.

Roses now vary in size from the tiniest miniatures, no more than 25cm/10in in height, to massive, sprawling ramblers, which may achieve 30m/100ft if left to their own devices. Almost without exception they are valued for their beautiful, often richly fragrant blooms, but many also have foliage that is attractive in its own right as well as providing an admirable foil for the flowers.

Roses offer an extraordinary diversity of habit: there are upright or arching shrubs; dense, thicket-forming bushes; and trailing and scrambling ramblers and climbers.

While not everyone would aspire to a country cottage with roses scrambling around the front door, the diversity of rose form and habit means that there is a rose to suit every garden, traditional or ultra-modern, from the largest plot to the smallest balcony. Some of these choices are described on the pages that follow, with advice on the care of your roses to ensure that they continue to reward you with colour and scent for years to come.

A History of the Rose

For centuries the rose has been a significant symbol, often adopted by royalty as an emblem. It is a well-known flower, recognized by gardeners and non-gardeners alike. Probably a native of the northern hemisphere, roses have been carried by settlers all over the world, where they have adapted and flourished. Now the world's most beloved flower, this remarkably varied species has a rich and colourful history.

■ RIGHT
The soft pink flowers of the gallica rose 'Duchesse de Montebello' are well loved for their sweet scent.

Roses through the centuries

Prized, cherished and fought over for centuries, roses now grow all over the world, although they are almost certainly indigenous to the northern hemisphere. Rose fossils, millions of years old, have been found only north of the equator, suggesting that those species now growing in South Africa, South America and Australia were taken there by immigrants.

Roses in ancient times

The wild rose was most certainly enjoyed by early people for its sweet petals and tasty hips, and rose cultivation probably began around 5,000 years ago in China and Persia (modern Iran). In antiquity the rose was regarded as the sacred flower of Venus, and Herodotus, writing about 430 BC, mentioned 60-petalled roses in the gardens of King Midas. In the *Iliad*, Homer's epic composed around 700 BC, the poet tells how Achilles' shield was decorated with roses to celebrate his victory over Hector and that the goddess Aphrodite anointed Hector's body with 'ambrosial oil of roses' before it was embalmed.

The roses mentioned by the Greek historians were almost certainly *Rosa gallica*, the ancestor of numerous European roses and so named by Linnaeus in 1753. *R. gallica* var. *officinalis* (syn. *R. officinalis*), which is also known as the apothecary's rose, the crimson damask rose, the red rose of Lancaster and Provins rose, was the main source of rose oil and medicinal preparations in Europe until roses from the Far East were introduced.

The early Christian church condemned roses as a symbol of depravity, and with some reason, since Nero's obsession with the flowers is widely believed to have contributed to the fall of the Roman Empire. The emperor's excesses were notorious, and it is said that tonnes of roses were required for the numerous banquets he gave. Vast quantities of petals were showered over people at orgies – it is said that at least one participant suffocated – and baths filled with pure rose water were offered to all the guests.

Roses symbolized success in Roman times, and consequently peasants came to believe that it was more profitable to grow roses than corn, a disastrous misconception that was noted by the poet Horace and other contemporary writers.

■ RIGHT
One of the best known and most ancient of all historic roses, *Rosa gallica* var. *officinalis*, was widely grown for its scent in the Middle Ages.

■ BELOW
Adopted by the House of York as its emblem in 15th-century England, *Rosa × alba* is still grown in gardens today. This is *R. × alba* 'Alba Semiplena', a semi-double variety grown in some parts of the world for the production of the essential oil, attar.

The Middle Ages

Little information exists about the cultivation of roses in Europe until about AD400, when the Church adopted the white *R. × alba* as the emblem of the Virgin Mary, who is called the 'rose without thorns'. St Ambrose, who died in AD397, recounted the legend that the rose grew without thorns until the Fall of Man.

In 1272, on his return from the eighth Crusade, Edward of England (later Edward I), ordered that rose trees should be planted in the gardens surrounding the Tower of London, and he chose a golden rose as his own symbol.

It is possible that the returning crusaders were responsible for the introduction to Europe of *R. × damascena* (the damask rose). By the end of the 15th century *R. × damascena* var. *semperflorens* (syn. *R. × damascena* var. *bifera*) was growing in English gardens. This rose, known as the autumn damask rose, the rose of Castille, the rose of Paestum and, from its French name 'Quatre Saisons', the four seasons rose, was the first grown in Europe to produce two crops of flowers every summer.

It is debatable if *R. gallica* was brought to England by the Romans or at a later date by the returning crusaders, but the red *R. gallica* var. *officinalis* was chosen as the emblem of the House of Lancaster in the prolonged struggle against the House of York (which adopted *R. × alba*) during the bitter Wars of the Roses in the 15th century.

The marriage of Henry Tudor (later Henry VII) and Elizabeth of York in 1486 finally united the factions. Their emblem was a white rose in the centre of a red rose entwined with a crown. Since that time the British royal family has adopted the rose as its own.

By the end of the 16th century *R. foetida*, known as the Austrian briar or Austrian yellow rose, had been introduced into Europe from Persia (now Iran), and *R. moschata*, the musk rose, was certainly favoured by the court of Henry VIII.

European roses were taken to the New World by the Pilgrim Fathers, the dissenters who fled religious persecution in Europe in 1620, and by the mid-17th century they were being grown in many gardens in Massachusetts. North America already had its own species, *R. virginiana* (syn. *R. lucida*) and *R. carolina*. Another species, *R. setigera*, the prairie rose, was later to produce some vigorous rambler cultivars, including the pale pink 'Baltimore Belle', which is still famous in the United States, and the climber 'Long John Silver', which bears fragrant, pure white flowers.

■ BELOW
Rosa × odorata 'Pallida', the old blush China rose, is one of the original China roses and was one of the most important introductions, bringing repeat-flowering genes to the modern rose. Its scent and long flowering season ensure that it is still planted by rose lovers.

New varieties

Until the process of hybridization was completely understood in the 19th century, new rose varieties were the results of natural crosses or sports (mutations), which were carefully chosen and nurtured by gardeners and nurserymen.

Dutch breeders pioneered work in Europe in the 17th century, working on *R. × centifolia*, which was called the cabbage rose because of the 'hundred-leaved' flowers. Moss roses first appeared around the mid-18th century as a sport from *R. × centifolia*. Rose breeding was also given tremendous impetus by the patronage of the Empress Josephine, the wife of Napoleon Bonaparte. Between 1803 and 1814 she commissioned botanists and nurserymen from all over the world to discover and breed new roses for her garden at Malmaison near Paris, where she eventually grew more than 250 varieties.

■ ABOVE
Introduced in 1932, 'The Fairy' is one of the oldest ground-cover roses. It is usually a healthy plant, with blooms from late summer to early autumn.

Far East introductions

The Chinese had been growing roses for thousands of years before they began to reach European growers in the late 18th century. Around 1781 a pink rose, sometimes known as the old blush China rose (now thought to be *R. × odorata* 'Pallida'), was planted in the Netherlands and was soon taken to Britain. In 1792 a captain of the British East India Company returned home with a red form of the same rose, which he had found growing in Calcutta, and it was named *R. semperflorens* or 'Slater's Crimson China'. Between them, these two roses are responsible for the remontant or repeat-flowering qualities in most modern roses.

At the beginning of the 19th century the flowers known as tea roses arrived on the ships of the British East India Company – their main cargo was tea, which probably accounts for the common name of these roses. They became fashionable in Europe, but because many of them are tender the Victorians grew them in grand conservatories, along with other exotic flowers brought back by explorers and botanists from all parts of the British Empire.

■ BELOW

'Souvenir de la Malmaison', first introduced in 1843, bears beautiful and strongly scented flowers in soft powder pink. There are also climbing and bush forms of this famous old Bourbon rose.

East meets West

One of the first marriages between a rose from the West and one from the East was probably a cross between *R.* × *damascena* var. *semperflorens*, the autumn damask, and a red China rose, which was probably obtained from France by the 2nd Duchess of Portland, an enthusiastic rose collector of the late 18th century. The Portland roses, as they came to be known, were very popular in the early 1800s. Although few survive today, they are ideal for growing in containers and are prized for their perfume and ability to flower throughout the summer.

Meanwhile, at around the same time in Charleston, South Carolina, a rice-grower called John Champney crossed a musk rose, *R. moschata*, with a China rose, 'Parson's Pink' (now known as *R.* × *odorata* 'Pallida'), which had been a gift from his friend and neighbour, Philippe Noisette. He gave the new seedling to Noisette, who made more crosses and sent both seed and plants to his brother, Louis, who was a nurseryman in Paris. The first seedlings were called 'Rosier de Philippe Noisette', a long name that came to be shortened to 'Noisette'.

'Noisette Carnée' (syn. 'Blush Noisette') is still widely grown, and so too is the beautiful 'Madame Alfred Carrière', one of the few climbing roses that can tolerate being grown against a north-facing wall.

Bourbon roses also made their appearance during this period. These began as a cross between *R.* × *odorata* 'Pallida', the old blush China rose, and *R.* × *damascena* var. *semperflorens*, the autumn damask rose, found growing in rose hedges on the Île de Bourbon (now called Réunion), an island in the Indian Ocean. Many of these shrub roses are still available, including 'Louise Odier' (syn. 'L'Ouche', 'Madame de Stella'), 'Souvenir de la Malmaison' (syn. 'Queen of Beauty and Fragrance') and the much-prized, thornless 'Zéphirine Drouhin'.

The modern rose

Throughout the 19th century hybrid perpetuals were introduced as a result of breeding between Chinas, Portlands, Bourbons and noisettes. The birth of what is considered to be the first modern rose, the large-flowered or hybrid tea rose, took place in Lyon in France in 1867 with the introduction of Jean-Baptiste Guillot's 'La France'. These new breed of roses satisfied gardeners' demands for neat, repeat-flowering and truly hardy shrubs with elegant and delicate flowers.

In the mid-18th century a wild rambler, *R. multiflora*, had been introduced from Japan. In the hands of 19th-century breeders it was to become the parent of the numerous cluster-flowered or floribunda roses that are grown today.

Most rose breeders of the 20th century have concentrated their efforts on floribunda and large-flowered (hybrid tea) roses, in colours echoing current tastes in fashion. Since the late 1960s there has also been a steady increase in the number of smaller shrubs for tiny gardens, patios and pots.

At the same time, a new breed of roses, evocative of Dutch old masters and the romantic paintings of Pierre Joseph Redouté (1759–1840), has been introduced by the British rose grower David Austin. He has raised roses that may be described as some of the finest reproductions, growing no more than 1.2m/4ft tall but with all the charm and scent of the classic roses of the past, crossing damasks and gallicas with modern shrub roses. Now owners of even the smallest garden may enjoy the delights of roses that the Empress Josephine would have considered for her garden.

■ LEFT
An outstanding modern shrub rose, 'L.D. Braithwaite' has all the charm of the old-fashioned roses.

■ OPPOSITE
'Dawn Chorus' is a hybrid tea rose with large, lightly scented, double, vivid orange flowers, with yellow petal reverses. The leaves are dark green with a red tinge. Flowers are produced in abundant clusters continuously throughout the summer, making this a good choice for bedding.

Roses Around the Garden

Roses are one of the best-loved plants of gardening enthusiasts around the world. Even a solitary rose makes a wonderful focal point in any part of the garden. On the following pages we look at some of the planting methods that will inspire you to ever-greater creativity. A wide variety of other plants can be combined with roses to blend in subtly or to highlight a contrast. Roses can also be enjoyed indoors, cut fresh from the garden, or dried for longer-lasting beauty.

■ RIGHT

The centifolia hybrid 'Fantin-Latour' flowers for much of the summer. This rose was introduced about 1900 and named after Henri Fantin-Latour, the French flower painter.

Where to grow roses

Roses are often grown in dedicated beds or in areas of the garden devoted solely to them, but they are very versatile plants that can be used imaginatively all around the garden. The following pages show some of the interesting and beautiful ways in which roses can be used.

Some rose enthusiasts prefer to create a rose garden in which few other plants feature, but there is a risk that such a strategy will leave the garden looking bare for part of the year. Other gardeners are put off planting more roses simply because of the short period of interest with some types, especially the once-flowering climbers and ramblers and some of the species and old-fashioned roses.

By selecting the right rose varieties for your garden, however, and using them creatively, it is possible to enjoy all the charm and beauty of roses without sacrificing any of the delights of your garden, year round.

■ ABOVE
The yellow floribunda shrub 'Chinatown' looks perfect in this mixed border.

■ RIGHT
Use climbers and ramblers to clothe otherwise boring fences and walls. Even when flowering is over, the foliage will act as a pleasing green screen for the rest of summer and into autumn. Here 'Madame Alfred Carrière', which continues to flower intermittently into autumn, is doing a magnificent job enhancing a boundary.

■ ABOVE
The clever positioning of a rose with an urn can lend structure to the planting and provide a pleasing contrast of form. This is 'Golden Celebrations', a modern shrub.

Purists may prefer their roses unadulterated, but most gardeners appreciate other plants, too, and one plant can often be used to enhance another. A rambling rose such as 'Wedding Day' climbing through a flowering cherry will drape the branches with creamy white flowers a month or two after the cherry blossom is over, giving two displays instead of one.

Clematis are compatible with roses, and they are often used together. A late-flowering clematis growing through a climbing or rambling rose will double the flowering capacity of a given space. Alternatively, a clematis that flowers at the same time as the rose can provide a stunning contrast of colours. Prune the clematis hard back in early spring.

Roses can be used together with other shrubs in shrub or mixed borders, and they can be used as hedges, flowering ground cover or even as container plants. In recent years breeders have created more versatile varieties with a wider range of uses and longer flowering periods, opening up many possibilities for using them all around the garden.

■ ABOVE
Climbing roses can soften and disguise harsh structures such as garden sheds. This is the fragrant and almost thornless 'Blush Rambler'.

■ ABOVE
Shrub roses look perfectly in place in a shrub or mixed border, and ramblers, climbers or pillar roses can be grown up supports to give height to the bed.

Happy marriages

For some stunning effects, try interplanting your roses with other plants that make happy combinations of colour and form. Purists may consider that this detracts from the roses, but as a garden feature roses can be enhanced by what you plant with them.

Pansies (*Viola* spp.) provide a simple solution if you want to cover the ground between the roses, especially in winter and spring when the roses are not in leaf. In summer they will find it difficult to compete in the shade, except at the edge of the border. Polyanthus (primulas) are also useful for spring colour.

In summer, when the roses are in bloom, their companions need to be stronger and bolder plants. Annual grasses provide an eye-catching contrast and are easily planted among existing roses, but choose a variety of grass that does not grow taller than the rose. Lavenders (*Lavandula* spp.) and catmints (*Nepeta* spp.), with their blue, lavender or purple flowers, are popular companions, but they are permanent features in the bed, and the spacing of the roses should allow for both plants.

It is worth experimenting with the unexpected, such as yellow day lilies (*Hemerocallis* cvs.) with yellow roses or pink gypsophila (baby's breath) interplanted among pink roses.

Always bear in mind that for tiptop roses you will need to feed, spray and, with some roses, regularly deadhead them. Plants that make rose cultivation difficult may mean some sacrifice of quality of bloom.

■ LEFT
Shrub roses and even ramblers are ideal for mixed borders if they can be given space to grow to their full potential. In this mainly white border, the white ramblers 'Félicité et Perpétue', 'Bobbie James' and 'Adélaïde d'Orléans' blend in beautifully among the other plants.

■ OPPOSITE
Clematis make ideal partners for roses, and here one acts as a bridge between 'Madame Alfred Carrière' and 'Bobbie James'. Clematis can be chosen to flower at the same time or to extend the period of interest by blooming later. If the clematis is to grow through the rose itself, where its stems will become entwined, selecting a late-flowering variety, which will need to be cut back hard in early spring, will make the task of pruning easier.

Beautiful beds

Many roses, especially large-flowered (hybrid tea) and cluster-flowered (floribunda) varieties, look best when massed in a rose bed. Where space is unrestricted, whole beds of a single variety can look stunning, especially when fragrance matches the perfection of bloom. Beds of mixed roses can also be very pleasing, but for impact plant in groups of about five plants of each variety and select varieties that harmonize well in terms of size and habit as well as colour.

Rose beds are most appropriate in a formal rose garden, with rectangular or circular beds set into the lawn, ideally with pergolas or arches clothed with climbers and ramblers. This kind of garden is a rose lover's paradise, especially if it is set with suitably positioned seats surrounded by fragrance. Many enthusiasts willingly forgo other plants for such bliss and beauty.

Floribundas are ideal for beds designed to be viewed from a distance, where a mass of blooms over a long period is more important than the quality of individual flowers. Beds of large-flowered (hybrid tea) roses generally have less impact from a distance, and flowering can be more uneven, especially where there are many varieties in the same bed. This is irrelevant for those rose lovers who prefer to savour the beauty of individual blooms.

Many modern gardens are too small for formal rose beds set in a large lawn, but there is plenty of scope for patio beds. Choose low-growing floribunda varieties – these are sometimes described as patio roses – for small beds set into the patio. Patio and miniature roses are also ideal for raised beds, where they can replace seasonal bedding plants. Although the initial investment is greater, the money you save on seasonal bedding will recover the cost of the roses over a few seasons.

■ LEFT
Rose beds have more impact if they are densely planted. Here, ground roses are combined with catmint along a path, while a profusion of climbing roses forms a stunning background on a pergola.

■ OPPOSITE
A formal rose garden is the ideal way to grow roses. Both visual impact and scent are concentrated, and it is a magical place to sit on a hot summer's day. Large rose beds such as this have space for many different kinds of rose, but even in a small rose garden it is important to use pergolas or frames for climbers to provide the essential element of height.

Border beauties

Roses are ideal border plants, whether they are grown in mixed plantings or in an area specifically dedicated to roses. Many varieties have a long flowering season that will outperform most other flowering shrubs, and, of course, they contribute the special charm of their fragrance.

If limited space in your garden makes it impossible for you to create formal rose beds cut into the lawn, it is usually possible to create a rose border. Instead of filling the area with herbaceous plants, pack it with roses of all kinds and colours. The border will look spectacular in early and mid-summer and will continue to provide pockets of interest right through until autumn.

Use shrub roses and pillar roses at the back of the border, modern shrub roses and the taller floribundas towards the centre, and compact floribundas and large-flowered (hybrid tea) types towards the front, with some of the long-flowering ground-cover roses as an edging. A kaleidoscope of colour works best with this kind of rose border and enables many varieties to be grown.

Rose borders are ideal for old-fashioned and modern shrub roses, many of which are too tall or bushy for formal rose beds. These roses also have a more informal shape, which is appropriate for a shrub border.

Use shrub roses to transform an existing shrub border that looks tired and rather dull, perhaps one that has large shrubs at the back that are grown largely for their foliage. Shrub roses planted in front of large, established shrubs will bring the border to life in summer, and the foliage behind makes a pleasing backdrop against which to view the roses. Species roses, especially the tall-growing kinds such as *Rosa moyesii*, which is grown for its decorative hips, and *R. sericea* subsp. *omeiensis* f. *pteracantha* (syn. *R. omeiensis* f. *pteracantha*), the winged thorn rose, which is grown mainly for its spectacular thorns, are also ideal in this situation.

If there is no space for a formal rose garden or rose border, integrate as many roses as possible into a mixed border. If you can make the border a viewpoint from an arbour of roses, or from a sitting area framed by roses, so much the better.

■ RIGHT

A plain, dark green hedge makes a good background against which to view a rose border. Pale colours, such as the flowers of the shrub rose 'Dapple Dawn', show up particularly well.

■ LEFT

Use ramblers, climbers and other tall roses at the back of a rose border. This will take the eye right to the back of the border, and the extra height makes sure that the feature is a focal point, even from a distance.

■ ABOVE

Try to incorporate a sitting area in the garden where you can linger to admire your rose border. Frame it with fragrant roses, perhaps using climbing roses to create a sense of enclosure like this. Use roses as a unifying theme to link different parts of the garden.

Hedges and boundaries

Garden walls and fences are essentially functional – that is, they are there to define the boundaries of the garden, to keep in children and pets and to keep out intruders. For a rose lover they are also a wonderful opportunity to plant more roses.

Walls and fences represent golden opportunities for planting climbing and rambling roses. Climbers can be planted against tall walls, while ramblers are a better choice for lower walls and fences. Even tall climbers and ramblers will, however, spread horizontally along a fence if they cannot grow upwards.

Fix horizontal supports 45–60cm/18–24in apart and train as many shoots as possible along these. New shoots will grow from this framework of horizontal branches to cover most of the wall or fence; whereas if all the shoots are allowed to grow upwards most of the flowers will be bunched together at the top and then simply tumble down over each other.

A rose hedge

Although roses can make beautiful boundaries and are ideal for an internal dividing hedge within a garden, they will not provide the year-round sense of privacy that an evergreen hedge of, say, privet or yew will impart. The thorny stems will deter some intruders and animals, but a rose hedge is best regarded as an ornamental feature.

Given these limitations, roses can make some of the best flowering hedging, blooming for far longer than most shrubs, and they sometimes have the bonus of scent. Few other hedges can match the rose for colour, length of flowering period and fragrance. Traditional choices are *Rosa rugosa* (sometimes called the hedgehog rose) and its varieties, such as 'Scabrosa', or the hybrid musk roses 'Cornelia' and 'Penelope'.

All of these roses will make a hedge 1.2m/4ft or more tall. For a smaller hedge try 'Ballerina', a lower growing polyantha hybrid musk with pink-flushed white flowers. The hydrangea-like clusters of musk-scented flowers are borne over a long period throughout the summer.

■ RIGHT
To obtain extra height for the more vigorous roses a trellis can be erected on top of a wall. When well-trained, they will present a backdrop of colour against which to view the border in front and below.

■ BELOW

Brick walls make an ideal background against which to view climbing roses, and in return the flowers soften the harshness of too much brickwork.

Tall floribunda roses also make pretty hedges, although they are less substantial than the shrub roses already mentioned. For that reason, it is best to plant them in a double, staggered row. Pleasing varieties for this purpose are 'Eye Paint' (syn. 'Maceye', 'Tapis Persan'), which has red flowers with white centres, 'Margaret Merril' (syn. 'Harkuly'), which has fragrant white flowers, 'Masquerade', whose flowers change from yellow to pink to dark red, and 'Southampton' (syn. 'Susan Ann'), which has apricot-orange flowers.

A rose hedge will be informal in profile and should not be clipped to a neat outline with shears.

Remember that rose hedges must not be neglected and allowed to become overgrown, especially those that border a public footpath. Roses with long, thorny shoots that catch on passers-by soon lead to disputes. Plant the roses a little further into the garden and not right at the edge so that they do not overhang a path.

Carpets of colour

Roses sound unpromising as ground-cover plants, but there are varieties able to create a carpet of colour that will look beautiful all summer long. They could be used to transform an area of neglected ground or a steep bank that is difficult to cultivate.

Some of the older ground-cover roses can be disappointing – they can be too tall for a small area and their flowering season is sometimes short. These criticisms, however, cannot be levelled against many of the compact ground-cover roses that have been bred in recent years. These literally form a carpet of blooms.

Roses will not create an impenetrable barrier against weeds, as some of the more traditional evergreen ground-cover shrubs do, but weeds are least active while the roses are dormant and devoid of foliage. Roses can therefore be quite effective weed suppressors if the ground is thoroughly cleared of weeds before planting and then mulched. The best way to be sure of eliminating weeds is to plant the roses through a mulching sheet.

The term 'ground-cover rose' is used to describe varieties with very different habits. Some are, indeed, ground hugging, but others are relatively tall and arching. Some have a spread of about 60cm/2ft, while others may reach 3m/10ft or more across. If you are considering a ground-cover rose, always make sure that the size and growth habit are appropriate for your garden. All these roses have their place in the garden, but the right kind must be chosen for each situation. There are three broad categories into which most ground-cover roses fit, although a few fall between these main groupings.

First are the tall ground-cover roses with arching stems. This group includes 'Pink Bells' (syn. 'Poulbells') and 'Red Bells' (syn. 'Poulred'), which grow to little more than 1m/3ft tall but have a spread of about 1.2m/4ft or more. The plants are smothered in double flowers in mid- and late summer. Prune them like shrub roses, but concentrate on shortening any branches that want to grow vertically.

The second group contains tall ground-cover roses that are almost as wide as they are tall. 'Rosy Cushion' (syn. 'Interall'), which has single, pink flowers; 'Smarty' (syn.

■ RIGHT
'Sussex' is a vigorous ground-cover rose that produces masses of apricot-pink flowers from early summer to autumn. It can be used in borders or in containers.

'Intersmart'), which has single, rose-madder flowers; 'Surrey' (syn. 'Korlanum'), which has double, pink flowers carried over a long period; and 'Sussex' (syn. 'Poulave'), which has double, apricot-pink flowers, also borne over a long period, fall into this category. Prune them in the same way as those with arching stems.

The final group consists of those varieties that spread wider than their height and that usually creep along the ground. It includes such roses as 'Pink Flower Carpet' (syn. 'Flower Carpet', 'Noatraum'), which has double, bright pink flowers over a long period; 'Grouse' (syn. 'Immensee', 'Korimro', 'Lac Rose'), which has single, pale pink flowers in mid- to late summer and which grows to about 60cm/2ft high but spreads to 3m/10ft or more; 'Kent' (syn. 'Poulcov', 'Pyrenees', 'White Cover'), which bears semi-double, white flowers; and *R.* × *jacksonii* 'Max Graf' (syn. 'Max Graf'), which has single, pink flowers and which ultimately grows to about 2.4m/8ft across. Other good choices are 'Nozomi' (syn. 'Heideröslein'), which has single, white-flushed pink flowers; 'Pheasant' (syn. 'Heidekönigin', 'Kordapt'), which has double, pink flowers borne in mid- to late summer and spreads to about 3m/10ft; and 'Snow Carpet' (syn. 'Maccarpe'), which has double, creamy white flowers. All these require minimal pruning other than to shorten the longest stems to restrain their spread.

■ ABOVE
'Kent' is a compact miniature rose that forms a carpet of pure white flowers from summer to autumn. It can also be grown to cascade from tall containers.

Roses as cut flowers

■ LEFT
Plunge freshly cut roses up to their necks in cool water for a few hours before arranging.

Beautiful at all stages, roses are the archetypal flower arranger's flower. They look stunning as tightly scrolled buds, at the height of their elegance just before opening, or as voluptuous flowers. The colour range is probably unmatched by any other flower, whether you are looking for brilliant whites, delicate creams and pastels or strong, vibrant reds, yellows and oranges. They last well, both in water and in florist's foam, and they are, of course, the traditional choice for buttonholes.

Whether you are buying roses or cutting them from the garden, always choose those in the very best condition. Reputable florists, supermarkets and flower stalls take pride in their flowers, selling only good quality blooms and having the knowledge and experience to keep them that way.

If you are cutting roses from the garden, it is best to gather them as early in the day as possible, when

ROSES FOR ARRANGING

Most roses provide good cut flowers, but the following are some of the longest lasting.

Pink
- 'Blue Moon'
- 'City of London'
- 'Double Delight'
- 'Escapade'
- 'Hannah Gordon'
- 'Julia's Rose'
- 'My Choice'
- 'Paul Shirville'
- 'Royal Highness'
- 'Savoy Hotel'
- 'Sexy Rexy'
- 'The Queen Elizabeth'

Red
- 'Alec's Red'
- 'Alexander'
- 'Big Purple'
- 'Fragrant Cloud'
- 'Ingrid Bergman'
- 'Papa Meilland'
- 'Precious Platinum'
- 'Red Ace'
- 'Red Devil'
- 'Royal William'

Orange
- 'Just Joey'
- 'Peek A Boo'
- 'Rosemary Harkness'
- 'Whisky Mac'

Yellow
- 'Allgold'
- 'Anne Harkness'
- 'Arthur Bell'
- 'Dutch Gold'
- 'Grandpa Dickson'
- 'Peace'
- 'Princess Michael of Kent'
- 'Sheila's Perfume'

White
- 'Elina'
- 'Elizabeth Harkness'
- 'Iceberg'
- 'Margaret Merril'
- 'Pascali'
- 'Polar Star'

PREPARING ROSES FOR A VASE ARRANGEMENT

1 After choosing the vase, cut off any leaves that will fall below the water level, because these will rot and cause the water to become stagnant.

2 Use a very sharp knife or pair of scissors to cut the stem diagonally to ensure maximum uptake of water. If thorns have to be removed because the roses are being used in a bouquet, use sharp scissors to cut them off, but not too close to the stem.

3 Add a proprietary flower food to the water in the vase to prolong the life of cut flowers and help to keep the water in the vase clear. It is sometimes possible to revive wilted roses by cutting the stems very short.

plant tissues are at their most turgid after the night dew. To increase your options when arranging, cut them with as long a stem as possible, cutting just above a leaf joint. For the longest lived arrangements, they should be still in bud but with the sepals fully reflexed. Immediately on cutting, stand the stems in fresh, deep water until you are ready to arrange them.

If you are buying roses, make sure that they are well wrapped to avoid excess evaporation and to protect their delicate petals. For long journeys, if practicable, it is best to put them in a bucket of water; alternatively, ask the retailer to cover the ends of the stems with damp paper. As soon as you reach home, give the flowers a long drink by standing them in deep, tepid water for at least an hour.

If you are arranging in water, begin by removing from the lower part of the stem all the leaves that would otherwise be below water. If left, they may rot, shortening the life of the arrangement and creating an unpleasant smell. Trim the base of the stems with a slanting cut. This provides the maximum area for the uptake of water and makes the stems easier to insert in plastic or florist's foam. Rose stems should never be crushed with a hammer, as some people suggest. This method destroys the delicate plant cells and makes the stalk less efficient in taking up water. It also encourages the spread of bacterial infection.

Opinions also differ about rose thorns. Some writers suggest that they can be removed by scraping a knife down the stems or, if the stems

■ LEFT
An airlock or bacterial infection can cause roses to wilt; it may be possible to revive them by cutting the stems very short.

are ripe, by snapping off the thorns with the finger and thumb. However, research has shown that bacteria may invade the gases left in the stem where the thorns are cut off, so it is better to remove the thorns only if the roses are going to be carried in a posy or bouquet when they might prick someone's hands.

Bacteria block the stems and cause the drooping heads so often experienced with shop-bought roses. You can avoid this problem by always using scrupulously clean vases, removing all leaves below the water level and adding commercially formulated flower food. This simple powder contains the correct amount of a mild and completely harmless disinfectant, which inhibits bacterial growth, together with the sugar that feeds the roses and encourages the flowers to mature and open. If flower flood is added to the water it is unnecessary to change it, but it may need topping up in warm weather. Although many people have their own recipes for increasing the longevity of cut roses – lemonade, aspirin, household bleach and so on – flower food is by far the most successful way of keeping roses at their best for longer.

For arrangements made using plastic foam, make holes for the rose and other stems with a wooden skewer. If you push the rose stem straight into the foam, particles of foam may become lodged in the base of the stem and prevent good water uptake, causing premature wilting. While arrangements in plastic foam often have great visual impact, they are usually shorter lived because it is impossible to feed the flowers after arranging. It is, however, possible to keep the arrangement fresh by periodically spraying with distilled water at room temperature.

If rose heads have wilted, either because of a bacterial infection or an airlock somewhere in the stem, it may be possible to revive them by wrapping them in strong paper and standing the stems in deep, tepid water for several hours, after first cutting at least 5cm/2in from the end of each stem. If this treatment fails, even more drastic action will be needed, and the roses will have to be cut very short in order to perk up their drooping heads.

■ ABOVE
Give first aid to wilting flower-heads by wrapping them securely in stiff paper and standing them in a large container of tepid water for a few hours.

Roses as dried flowers

■ BELOW
Drying roses at home is not difficult and it is a wonderful way to preserve the beauty of the flowers.

People have always wanted preserve the beautiful flowers and sweet scent of roses, and they have therefore been dried for as long as they have been cultivated. Rose petals have been used in pot-pourri or the whole stems in decorative arrangements when fresh flowers were scarce. The Elizabethans preserved roses by immersing them completely in dry sand and keeping them warm until all the moisture had been drawn out. In Victorian times, when houses were heated from open coal fires, which shortened the lives of fresh blooms, intricate dried arrangements were painstakingly created and then covered in glass domes to keep them free of dust. These rather contrived designs have lost their appeal in favour of looser, more natural arrangements, and contemporary designs using dried flowers have achieved new popularity.

The latest commercial method for drying roses is freeze-drying. The technique takes up to two weeks and requires specialized freezers, and it is therefore rather expensive, but the results are stunning. Dried roses retain all their original intensity of colour and, in some cases, even their fragrance. Freeze-dried flowers last for about five years before they begin to fade or disintegrate.

Air-drying is the most popular way of preserving roses at home. It is best for buds that are just about to open but still have their bud shape. They need to be hung somewhere that is well-ventilated, warm, dry and dark for a couple of weeks – a large airing-cupboard would be ideal. String them together washing-line-style to speed up the process and prevent any moisture being trapped between the flowers. Once they are completely dry, handle with care as the stems will be very brittle.

The petals will now have a delicate, faded tone. Try displaying a tight bunch of rosebuds packed together in a small terracotta pot for maximum impact. A gentle blow on the lowest setting of a hair-drier will usually be sufficient to remove most of the dust that settles on them.

Drying roses in a microwave oven is suitable for arrangements requiring short stems. Lay the flowers on greaseproof paper and put them into the microwave, which should be switched to its lowest setting. The roses will take only a very short time, and you should check them every minute to prevent over-cooking.

The third method is to use a desiccant such as silica gel, available from chemists and craft shops, or fine sand. Some scilica gels change colour as they absorb the moisture from the plant material. A desiccant is suitable for drying single flowers.

Classifying Roses

Rose classification has never been an exact science. Although the groups appear to be precisely defined horticulturally, the groupings are actually devised for the convenience of the gardener. Based on flowering patterns and habit of growth, the main groups are wild or species roses, old garden roses, early hybrids of European and Oriental roses, and modern roses.

 RIGHT

'Bobbie James' is a vigorous rambling rose with sweetly scented small white flowers.

Identifying rose groups

Over the years hybridization has made the botanical classification of roses complex, and it is more useful for gardeners to group them by growth and flowering habit. There are several thousand documented roses, including original species and scores of hybrids that have been bred during the last four centuries. Many more new rose varieties are introduced every year, and older hybrids are being rediscovered all over the world.

The world's rose societies have developed a horticultural classification that is broadly based on habit of growth and flowering patterns, and the main groups are wild or species roses, old garden roses, early hybrids of European and Oriental roses, and modern roses. In 1971 the World Federation of Rose Societies reclassified both ancient and modern roses into more clearly defined garden groups.Broadly speaking, the era of the modern rose began in 1867 with the introduction of the first hybrid tea (large-flowered) rose, 'La France', by the French grower Jean-Baptiste Guillot. This rose is still available from one or two specialist nurseries.

The categories described here are broadly accepted by the rose growing community, but there will always be a few plants included in one group that some growers may feel belong rightly in one of the others.

Wild or species roses

This group includes the species and those roses that are hybrids of them with features that clearly identify them as offspring of a particular species. They are generally vigorous and produce one flush of single flowers in early summer, often followed by decorative hips. One of the most popular wild rose hybrids is 'Dupontii' which has beautiful white flowers with golden stamens.

Old roses

When it comes to classifying old roses there are no hard-and-fast rules. Even the term 'old rose' is itself rather misleading, as this group often includes some modern hybrids that fit into this category as they have the grace and flower form that are associated with older roses.

With a few exceptions, old garden roses are the albas, gallicas, damasks, centifolias and moss roses, along with the Scotch or burnet roses (derived from *R. pimpinellifolia*) and the sweet briars (derived from *R. rubiginosa*).

■ LEFT
R. rugosa **has distinctive wrinked leaves and bright pink flowers, followed in autumn by large, rounded red hips.**

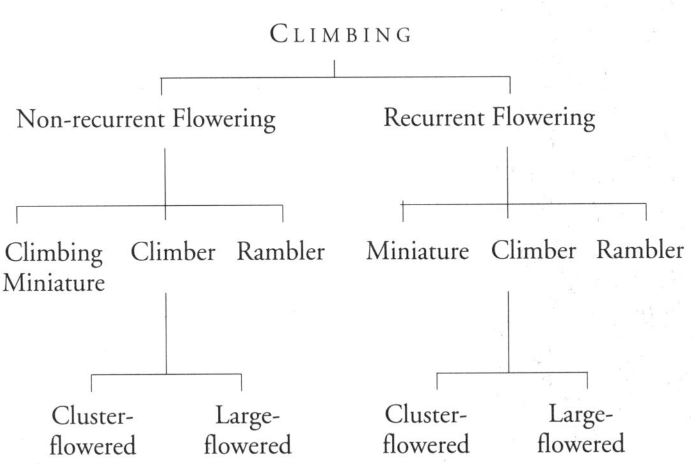

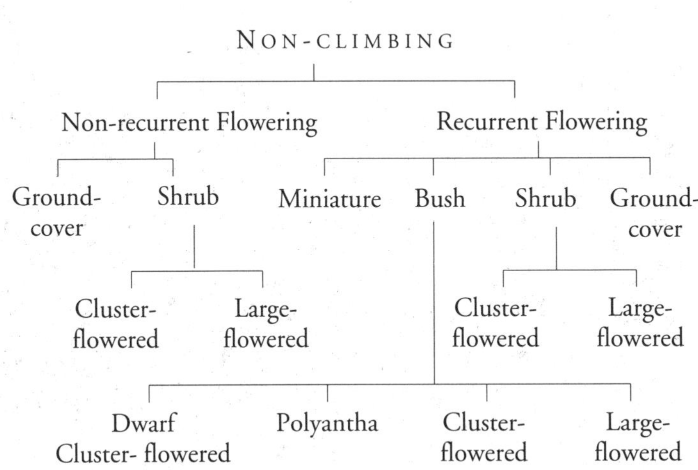

These shrubs, many of them intensely fragrant, vary considerably in size, habit, flower shape and colour.

The polyanthas – compact, hardy and relatively thornless shrubs and climbers – are also often (although not invariably) included with the old roses.

Early hybrids

The early European and Oriental hybrids are mostly repeat-flowering roses derived from crossings with *R. chinensis*, and include Chinas, Portlands, noisettes, Bourbons, tea roses and hybrid perpetuals.

■ RIGHT

The Bourbon rose 'Louise Odier' was introduced in 1851. It is still grown for its strongly scented, warm-pink flowers.

Alba

These large, long-lived, strong-growing roses have attractive grey-green foliage and produce a single flush of white or pale pink flowers in mid-summer. They will tolerate poor soil. Popular alba roses include 'Königin von Dänemark' (syn. 'Belle Courtisane') and 'Great Maiden's Blush' (syn. 'Cuisse de Nymphe').

Bourbon

A vigorous, usually repeat-flowering, rose which can also be trained as short climber. Some grow to over 3m/10ft, others remain low-growing and shrubby. Bourbon roses are sweetly scented and derive from a damask × China cross. 'Souvenir de la Malmaison' and 'Madame Isaac Pereire' are amongst the best known.

Centifolia

These lax shrubs have large, many-petalled flowers which weigh down the arching stems. The leaves are large, drooping and sometimes wrinkled. Centifolias are sometimes referred to as cabbage, Provence or Holland roses. A typical centifolia is *R.* × *centifolia* 'Cristata' (syn. 'Chapeau de Napoléon').

■ LEFT
Rosa odorata 'Mutabilis' is a China rose of unknown origin which displays beautifully subtle changes of colour as it ages.

China

A dainty, repeat-flowering shrub of light, open habit, with small, scented flowers and leaves. China roses are sometimes grown under glass in cold climates, since they are not fully hardy. 'Irène Watts', which has large, double flowers in a delicate shade of pink, is a China rose.

Damask

The lax, spreading, medium-sized to large shrubs usually bear highly scented flowers in clear colours. The leaves are typically greyish-green and have downy undersides. 'Madame Hardy', which has fully double, fragrant, white flowers, is among the most widely grown damask roses.

Gallica

Usually upright, although occasionally spreading, the compact shrubs have coarse leaves and flowers in deep shades of pink, rich crimson and purple. The group includes some striped roses. The lovely roses 'Tuscany Superb' and 'Charles de Mills' are in this group.

Hybrid Musk

Similar to the modern shrub rose, these have *R. moschata*, the musk rose, in their make-up. These roses were first bred between 1913 and 1926. One of the earliest introductions, the creamy white flowered 'Moonlight' (introduced in 1913) is still available.

Hybrid Perpetual

The vigorous shrubs, usually repeat-flowering, initially grow upright. Legginess tends to develop later, but the problem may be overcome by pegging down the overlong shoots. Popular hybrid perpetuals are 'Mrs John Laing' and 'Frau Karl Druschki' (syn. 'Reine des Neiges', 'Snow Queen', 'White American Beauty').

Moss

Closely allied to the centifolia roses, moss roses arose as sports of centifolias and damasks, but they are distinguished by the characteristic mossy growth on their stems and calyces. The old black rose 'Nuits de Young' has the typical brownish-green mossing on the stems.

Noisette

The first noisette rose was grown in Charleston, South Carolina in the early 1800s. It is believed to have resulted from a cross between the old blush China rose (*R.* × *odorata* 'Pallida') with a musk rose, *R. moschata*. These climbing roses usually have glossy leaves and fairly smooth stems. 'Madame Alfred Carrière', one of the best known and most widely grown of all climbing roses, is a noisette.

Polyantha

This group of roses is now more or less obsolete. They are tough and repeat flowering and produce trusses of small flowers. The beautiful rose 'Cécile Brünner' (syn. 'Mignon', 'Sweetheart Rose') is sometimes classified as a polyantha. These are the forebears of the modern cluster-flowered (floribunda) roses.

Portland

The result of a damask × gallica cross, Portland roses are similar to the Bourbon roses but repeat more reliably and make small plants. 'Madame Knorr' (syn. 'Comte de Chambord'), introduced in 1860, is still available and widely grown.

Rugosa

These tough, vigorous and very hardy plants have crinkled foliage and single to double flowers, which are succeeded by large, tomato-like hips.

The rugosas originated in the Far East and have not been used extensively in rose breeding in the West. Nevertheless, rugosa roses are easy to grow and are valued for their robust constitution and their ability to tolerate some shade. They can be used as hedging, as specimens, in the border or in light woodland. 'Blanche Double de Coubert', which was introduced as long ago as 1892, is still popular.

Scotch Roses

These roses are dense shrubs with *R. pimpinellifolia* (syn. *R. spinosissima*), the burnet or Scots rose, in their make-up. The stems are often prickly. 'Frühlingsmorgen' (syn. 'Spring Morning') is a pimpinellifolia hybrid.

Tea

The slender-stemmed tea roses flower repeatedly throughout the summer, although they are often weak-growing shrubs which may need the protection of glasshouses in cold climates. Slender, pointed buds are a feature of many of the modern, large-flowered roses that are derived from them and that are often known as hybrid teas.

WHAT'S IN A NAME?

Although almost thirty years have elapsed since the new classifications were recommended, both gardeners and growers tend to cling to the old names with which most are familiar. In many catalogues, on labels in rose gardens and in everyday conversation, cluster-flowered roses are still likely to be described as floribundas and large-flowered roses referred to as hybrid teas. Both terms are used for each type of rose in this book.

In addition to what might be regarded as the 'official' categories, catalogues sometimes describe varieties as 'patio roses'. These are low-growing cluster-flowered (floribunda) roses that are suitable for patio beds or containers. Some of the smaller patio roses are similar in size to the largest miniatures.

Catalogues sometimes use a grower's code name for the variety as well as the name under which it is widely known and distributed. For example, 'Sexy Rexy' is the selling name of 'Macrexy' (which was bred by McGredy), and 'Paul Shirville' is the selling name of 'Harqueterwife' (which was bred by Harkness). The breeder's name is a way of identifying a variety if the local name is changed when the rose is sold in different countries. It is also the name likely to be used during early trials, before the variety is released to the public.

■ BELOW
Ground-cover roses such as 'Red Bells' have a low, spreading habit and form dome-like mounds.

Modern roses

The suggestion that rose groupings are devised for the convenience of gardeners and are of little significance botanically is well illustrated by the categories used for modern roses. Some cluster-flowered (floribunda) roses – for instance, 'Chinatown' – are potentially large bushes that some growers prefer to define as shrub roses and treat accordingly. Some large-flowered (hybrid tea) roses have a tendency to produce smaller buds around the main bud, showing some of the characteristics of the cluster-flowered rose.

Modern roses are deciduous shrubs that bear their flowers on wood produced during the current season and on shoots emerging from the previous year's wood. In warm climates roses will grow virtually continuously, but in cold climates there is a period of winter dormancy. Roses generally benefit from pruning when they are dormant, usually early spring, to maintain a high proportion of young, productive growth.

Modern shrub roses are usually large, repeat-flowering shrubs that were bred after the advent of large-flowered (hybrid tea) and cluster-flowered (floribunda) roses.

Cluster-flowered Roses

Also known as floribundas. These sometimes large shrubs bear single to fully double flowers in clusters. The flowers usually open flat to reveal their stamens, producing dome-shaped heads. Cluster-flowered roses are a diverse group and can have a wide variety of uses around the garden: some can be grown as hedges or as specimens, whereas others are suitable for bedding or more informal planting schemes.

Dwarf Cluster-flowered Bush Roses

Also sometimes known as patio roses. Dwarf cluster-flowered bush roses are similar in style to cluster-flowered roses, but they are much smaller. Although they were bred specifically to be grown in containers, they are also good plants for patio beds, borders and low hedges.

Ground-cover Roses

Roses with a lax, trailing habit, they are closely allied to ramblers but are generally much smaller. Many have single flowers. Ground-cover roses can be used to cover banks or trail from raised beds. They are sometimes available as weeping standards.

Large-flowered Roses

Also known as hybrid teas. The shrubs are characterized by large flowers, usually carried singly but which sometimes grow in small clusters. They open from pointed buds usually to a high-centred, round or urn-shaped flower. Typically, the flowers are fully double, although there are a few varieties with single flowers. Many are suitable for bedding or mixed planting. A few large-flowered roses are stiff, rather gaunt plants, which are best grown solely for cut flowers.

Miniature Roses

These are compact plants, usually under 30cm/1ft high, carrying sprays of tiny flowers, which are often scentless. Miniature roses are versatile plants and can be grown in containers, to edge a border or in a rock garden. They are also sometimes sold as pot plants.

■ BELOW
The rich crimson 'Parkdirektor Riggers' is a good rose for growing up a pillar. It bears repeated flushes of crimson flowers.

Climbing roses

Unlike bush roses, climbing roses cannot be conveniently ascribed to distinct groups. They have a variety of ancestors and varying growth habits, which make them suitable for different garden uses. Habit – the way a rose (or any plant) grows – should be as important a consideration as flower colour and scent when choosing a rose for the garden but, unfortunately, is all too often overlooked. This section will help avoid some of the pitfalls.

Most climbing roses are deciduous, although a few, such as the vigorous 'Mermaid' and 'Albéric Barbier', are evergreen or semi-evergreen. In botanical and gardening terms they are divided into ramblers and climbers.

Rambling Roses

The rambling roses that are closely related to their wild ancestors – 'Seagull', 'Rambling Rector' and 'Wedding Day', for example – produce large trusses of small, single, usually highly fragrant flowers in a single flush around mid-summer on slender, flexible stems. Some are extremely vigorous indeed and must be given plenty of room.

A few rambling roses, however, such as 'Albertine', produce larger flowers, also in clusters, on stiffer, less flexible stems. All ramblers flower on wood that was produced the previous year. Some flower reliably on older wood. In some cases decorative hips follow in the autumn. After flowering, most produce large quantities of new wood from around the base of the plant. Ramblers usually need ample space to give of their best and are suitable for informal planting in a wild garden. They do not lend themselves to formal planting schemes and are less suitable than climbers for growing against walls.

Climbing Roses

This group of roses usually flowers twice, the first flush appearing around mid-summer, the second, lesser flush in early autumn. Some, such as 'Mermaid', have a main flush in summer followed by spasmodic flowering right up until the first frosts of winter. These flowers are produced in small trusses on the current season's growth.

Most roses are thorny. In some cases – 'Albertine' and 'Mermaid', for example – the thorns are viciously sharp, but other roses – for example, 'Zéphirine Drouhin' and 'Climbing Iceberg' – have stems which are virtually thornless.

Some climbing roses are more tolerant of shade than bush roses, reflecting the fact that many of the wild roses from which they are descended were woodland plants.

In response to the needs of gardeners with only limited space, most climbers that have been bred since 1949 are only moderately vigorous and in many cases grow no more than 5m/16½ft tall. Some have been developed to reach no more than 2.4m/8ft or less, and miniature climbers seldom exceed 2.1m/7ft.

Extensive breeding and cross-breeding by modern rose breeders have meant that all the varied flower forms of bush roses can be found among climbing roses, which gives the gardener extra choice.

■ BELOW – FROM TOP TO BOTTOM
Flower shapes: flat, cupped and rounded.

Flower shape

Most modern roses have many petals. Single flowers have eight or fewer petals; semi-double ones have 8–20 petals; double flowers have 20 or more petals, and fully double ones have 30 or more. Because of the double nature of most rose flowers and the sterility (or part sterility) of many, pollination in the garden seldom takes place, and hips are generally not produced.

Modern roses have stronger, richer colours than old roses, and their thicker petals are generally more rain resistant. They also have a longer flowering season, either in two distinct flushes (one around mid-summer, the other in late summer to autumn) or flower more or less continuously from summer until the first frosts.

Although this is a guide only, the flower shapes of roses are generally described as follows.

Flat
Single (with five petals) or semi-double (with ten petals) flowers open virtually flat, often revealing a prominent boss of stamens. A good example of an old rose with flat flowers is 'Dupontii'.

Cupped
Single to semi-double flowers with incurving petals that form a shallow to deep cup shape around the central stamens. *R. xanthina* 'Canary Bird' has beautiful yellow cupped flowers.

Rounded
Double or fully double flowers, with a rounded outline, formed by overlapping petals, which are usually of equal size and which form a bowl-shaped outline. 'Madame Grégoire Staechelin' (syn. 'Spanish Beauty') is a climbing rose with fully double rounded flowers.

Rosette
The low-centred, almost flat, semi- to fully double flowers are packed with many short, overlapping petals of uneven size. 'William Lobb' (syn. 'Duchesse d'Istrie'), first introduced in 1855, has large, double, rosette flowers.

Quartered rosette
Similar to the double or fully double rosette, but the petals are arranged in distinctive quarters within the flower. One of the best known roses with such flowers is 'Souvenir de la Malmaison', which bears scented, soft pink flowers.

■ BELOW – LEFT TO RIGHT
Flower shapes: rosette, quartered rosette and pompon.

Pompon

Double or fully double flowers, generally borne in clusters, are small, rounded and packed with many tiny petals. 'Pompon de Paris' (syn. *R. chinensis* 'Minima', 'Rouletii') is one of the smallest miniature roses but has – as its name suggests – beautiful pompon flowers.

High-pointed

The semi- to fully double flowers have a tight, high-pointed centre, as seen in many large-flowered (hybrid tea) roses. The patio rose 'Cider Cup' (syn. 'Dicladida') has high-pointed flowers in an unusual warm apricot-pink colour.

■ RIGHT – LEFT TO RIGHT
Flower shapes: urn-shaped and high-pointed.

Urn-shaped

Semi- to fully double blooms with incurved inner petals and more spreading outer petals. This is the characteristic shape of China and tea roses, which have long, slender, elegant buds that open to high-centred or urn-shaped flowers. A classic example of a China rose with urn-shaped flowers is 'Cécile Brünner'.

OLD ROSES

The *grandes dames* of the summer border and unsurpassed for their sumptuous flowers and heady fragrance, old roses still deserve a place in every garden. That they have endured is a tribute not only to their beauty but also to their ease of cultivation.

Old roses lend themselves to an informal, mixed, cottage style of planting that also incorporates other shrubs, as well as hardy perennials and summer-flowering bulbs. Many of them make large, spreading plants that look beautiful against some form of support, although you can allow them to grow over and through neighbouring shrubs. Some gallicas, Chinas and tea roses, however, grow no larger than 1.2m/4ft, which makes them suitable for the smallest garden.

■ PREVIOUS PAGE
Rosa × *alba* 'Alba Semiplena' has been grown since at least the 16th century.

■ RIGHT
The English rose 'Constance Spry' trained against a wall.

The history of old roses

What is an 'old' rose? Some define an old rose as one that was developed and grown before the First World War (1914–18), but the answer to this deceptively simple question is unfortunately not quite so clear cut. Indeed, it would be simpler to turn it on its head and ask what a modern rose is. By common consent, modern roses are the large-flowered and cluster-flowered roses (formerly hybrid teas and floribundas) that until recently made up the majority of roses in commerce. Given the fact that the first hybrid tea – 'La France' – appeared as long ago as 1867, it will be evident from the discussion below that many of the so-called old roses are a good deal younger than that.

Nowadays, the long and stately catalogue of old roses comprises various distinct groups: gallicas, damasks, albas, centifolias, mosses, Bourbons, Portlands, Chinas, hybrid perpetuals and teas. In this book we also include the attendant species or wild roses, rugosas, hybrid musks, modern shrub roses and English roses (for descriptions of each see Classification and flower shapes).

It is probably true to say that for as long as people have made gardens they have grown roses in them; indeed, it would be impossible to exaggerate the rose's importance as the *nonpareil* among garden plants, and its mystique transcends the usual cultural barriers.

Precisely when many of the individual groups arose is not known, but what is certain is that one of the first to be grown in gardens that is recognizable today is *Rosa gallica.* The influence of this rose is present in nearly all of the roses that are still big favourites today. A cross between this and *R. phoenicia* (or possibly *R. moschata*) resulted in *R.* × *damascena,*

■ OPPOSITE
R. × *damascena* var. *semperflorens*, sometimes called 'Quatre Saisons', is one of the oldest roses. It occasionally produces repeat flowers in autumn.

■ BELOW
One of the most ancient of roses, 'Old Blush China' also has one of the longest flowering seasons.

■ LEFT
A moss rose, showing the characteristic mossy stems and calyces.

the original damask. Further crosses and back-crosses occurred, and out of the melting-pot emerged the albas. Pliny the Younger, the great Roman letter writer, grew various kinds at his two country villas and the Romans introduced some of them into the rest of their western empire. Pliny also grew a rose he described as centifolia (literally, with a hundred leaves, although meaning petals), but this is thought to be a different rose to the centifolias we know today. These did not evolve until the 16th century.

The rose retained its supremacy throughout the medieval period and the Renaissance, and acquired both sacred and secular resonances. It was one of the celebrated plants in the gardens of Islam since it was believed to have been created from a bead of perspiration on the brow of Mohammed, and roses are recorded growing in the palace garden in Constantinople in the 16th century. In medieval Europe, roses came to be associated both with the Holy Spirit and the Virgin Mary. *R. gallica* var. *officinalis* had a commercial value and was known as the apothecary's rose because it was used as an ingredient in medicines, or as the Provins rose after the area of France where it was grown for perfume production.

In England, its flower was adopted as the badge of the House of Lancaster. The rival House of York used 'Alba Semiplena' (or possibly the British native *R. arvensis*), and Henry VII merged the two – heraldically speaking – to form the Tudor rose. Later, the double 'Alba Maxima' became the emblem of Bonnie Prince Charlie.

Botticelli used some artistic licence, since the rose is the quintessential flower of summer, when he painted his 'Primavera' – she who embodies Spring – wearing a dress decorated with roses; she also carries a bouquet of the same flowers.

Centifolias – sometimes called cabbage roses – were common in Holland and France, to the extent that they were sometimes known as Holland or Provence roses; they often appear in 17th-century Dutch flower paintings.

■ BELOW
Venus, patroness of flower gardens, oversees a mass planting of roses.

The moss rose, *R.* × *centifolia* 'Muscosa', which is distinguished by its mossy stems and calyces (the green segments that enclose the unopened bud), is a sport (a spontaneous mutation) of a centifolia that was first noticed in approximately 1720. At around the same time, China and tea roses began to arrive in Europe from the Far East. Initially attracting little interest other than as novelties, since they did not prove to be hardy in north European climates and thus had to be grown under glass, they contributed significantly to the explosion in rose breeding that occurred in the 19th century. Unfortunately, little is known of the history of these plants prior to their European debut.

The value of the tea and China roses as breeding material lay not only in their elegance, scent and colour but in the fact that they have an

■ BELOW

In late summer, the soft tones of border phlox blend beautifully with old roses.

■ RIGHT
The hybrid musk rose 'Penelope' is a glorious sight in full bloom.

extended flowering season: some produce two distinct flushes and others flower virtually non-stop through the summer. Earlier European groups produce one glorious crop of flowers in mid-summer then do not flower again. The so-called autumn damask (*R.* × *damascena* var. *semperflorens*), sometimes called 'Quatre Saisons', is an exception that squeezes out a few further blooms in autumn. Crosses between this and the Chinas resulted in the repeat-flowering Bourbon and Portland roses that became the new stars in the rose firmament. Further cross-breeding led to the hybrid perpetuals, which have a more dependable second flush. All of the modern repeat-flowering roses owe this characteristic to the Chinas.

It was in 19th-century France that rose breeding began in earnest, and it is from this period on that most of the old roses that we still grow today were bred. Their names read like a roll-call of the top brass and society beauties of the day: the Duc de Guiche, Président de Sèze, the Duchesse de Montebello and Madame Hardy. The vogue was started by the interest, indeed passion, of the Empress Josephine (1763–1814). At her country house of Malmaison she created what was virtually the first rose garden. Her 250 plants were recorded for posterity by the great botanical artist Pierre-Joseph Redouté. This was probably the rose's heyday – at least before the development of the hybrid teas and floribundas – but a number of mainly English rosarians kept the torch glowing into the 20th century. Among the prime movers were Gertrude Jekyll and the Revd Joseph Pemberton, who created the group of roses called hybrid musks, probably by crossing a musk rose with a tea or China rose. Vita Sackville-West grew many old roses in her garden at Sissinghurst and also fostered interest in them through her writings. More recently, David Austin developed a new group that he called English roses, which combine the style of the older groups with the repeat-flowering and robust habit of modern roses.

Old roses in the garden

Generally tough, hardy and free-flowering, old roses are splendid subjects for the garden, and all lend themselves to an informal, mixed, cottage style of planting that uses other shrubs, hardy perennials and summer bulbs. Many make large, rangy plants that may need some form of support (see Alternative ways of growing old roses), or you can allow them to flop over gracefully into neighbouring shrubs. There are some gallicas, Chinas and teas, however, that grow no larger than 1.2m (4ft) and are suitable for the smallest gardens.

Flower colours of the European types include white, all shades of pink, dusky red, crimson and purple; some flowers, such as *R. gallica* 'Versicolor' (commonly known as 'Rosa Mundi') and 'Variegata di Bologna' (Bourbon), are striped in a combination of these colours. Genes from the China and tea roses have widened the range to include yellow and soft orange, but on the whole the palette is one that we associate with old silks, chintzes and velvets. In some flowers, the colour changes as the flower ages, a good example being the gallica 'Belle de Crécy', whose rich lilac flowers gradually pale into tones of dove grey. On the whole, therefore, it is best to keep old roses away from other flowers that have strong clear colours, though for a bold contrast you could try the rich purple gallicas 'Cardinal de Richelieu' or 'Tuscany Superb' with a sulphur-yellow *Achillea* such as 'Gold Plate'.

Otherwise, for strong contrasts, it is probably better to think in terms of form rather than colour: the

■ LEFT
A ceanothus graciously supports an old rose and a late-flowering clematis.

■ OPPOSITE
A spectacular massed planting: a vigorous philadelphus forms the backdrop, while a mature Bourbon spreads its arching canes accommodatingly to fill the middle ground. Reliable hardy geraniums and *Dianthus* sport at their feet.

■ BELOW
The colour blue always provides a perfect foil for soft pink roses such as 'De Meaux'.

geometric shapes of alliums (*A. sphaerocephalon* or *A. giganteum*) are the perfect foil to the roses' lax habit, or try the strong verticals of foxgloves (*Digitalis purpurea*), in their white or apricot-pink forms, or the milky-blue or white Canterbury bells (*Campanula medium*), both biennials that are easily raised from seed. The perennial *C. lactiflora* would also work well, particularly the dusky pink variety 'Loddon Anna'.

For a less spiky, more integrated effect use easy border perennials, such as hardy geraniums, lady's mantle (*Alchemilla mollis*) or catmint (*Nepeta* × *faassenii*), all of which will blend with most old roses. Clouds of gypsophila (*G. paniculata*) or bronze fennel (*Foeniculum vulgare* 'Purpureum') will further soften the edges.

■ RIGHT
The flagon-shaped, vibrant red hips of *R. moyesii* make a stunning clash with purple *Thalictrum aquilegiifolium*.

If you are still concerned about colour clashes, add a few grey-leaved plants such as artemisia (especially *A. lactiflora*), lambs' ears (*Stachys byzantina*), sage (*Salvia officinalis*) or *Senecio* (now sometimes listed as *Brachyglottis*) 'Sunshine', though you will have to remove its ugly daisy-like flowers. In a large border, underplant a tall-growing rose such as the alba 'Great Maiden's Blush' with a hosta: the huge leaves of *H. sieboldiana* 'Elegans' would provide a sumptuous quilted cushion for the roses to rest on. For edging, tightly clipped box (*Buxus sempervirens* 'Suffruticosa') is traditional, but lavender, rosemary or the curry plant (*Helichrysum italicum*) would be more informal.

Besides the beauty of the flowers, and perhaps even above that, roses are prized for their scent. This can range from the delicate tang of a modern shrub such as 'Nevada', more apparent wafted on the air from a distance than close to, to the rich, crushed-berry fragrance of the Bourbon 'Madame Isaac Pereire'.

To create a voluptuous pot-pourri of scents, provide a backdrop of mock orange (*Philadelphus*), the flowering of which will coincide with the roses' main mid-summer flush. Underplant with old-fashioned pinks (*Dianthus*), such as the clove-scented 'Gran's Favourite' or 'Sops-in-Wine', the headily fragrant lily *Lilium regale* or the incense-scented annual tobacco flower, *Nicotiana alata*. Remember that the scents will be heaviest at dusk, particularly after a light shower.

If your roses are the kind that produce a single crop of flowers, for interest later in the season use them as props for late-flowering clematis. The rich purple 'Jackmanii', one of the most reliable, would look stunning entwined with the vibrant red hips of *R. moyesii* or any of the rugosas, particularly if the flame-red *Crocosmia* 'Lucifer', cannas, dahlias and orange annual nasturtiums (*Tropaeolum majus*) were planted as a supporting cast, bringing the curtain down on the rose season with a sensational chorus of colour.

Plant Directory

In the following gallery, roses are arranged alphabetically within categories as follows (for further information, see Classification and flower shapes)

Wild roses
Albas
Bourbons
Centifolias and mosses
Chinas and teas
Damasks
Gallicas
Other types

The height and spread cited in each case are what the rose can be expected to achieve on maturity given favourable conditions; they may vary depending on climate, season and soil type.

■ ABOVE
R. XANTHINA 'CANARY BIRD'

Wild rose of uncertain origin but assumed to be after 1907, the date of introduction of one of its possible parents, *R. xanthina* f. *spontanea*. It makes an arching shrub, 2.1m (7ft) high and as much across or bigger. In late spring, the canes are covered in cupped, single, scented, canary-yellow flowers with prominent stamens. The leaves are fern-like. *R. xanthina* 'Canary Bird', one of the earliest roses to flower, tolerates some shade. It is sometimes available as a grafted standard.

Wild roses

■ RIGHT
'DUPONTII'

Wild rose hybrid, introduced around 1817, that forms a spreading shrub 2.1m (7ft) high and across. In summer, the large, single, creamy white flowers open flat to reveal yellow stamens. The matt grey-green leaves are downy beneath. 'Dupontii' was grown by Empress Josephine and illustrated by Redouté as *R. damascena subalba*.

Albas

■ BELOW

'ALBA MAXIMA'

Alba rose, dating from at least the 15th century, reaching a height of 2m (6ft) with a spread of 1.5m (5ft). Somewhat untidy, cupped, double, very fragrant flowers, tinged pink on opening in summer but fading to creamy white, are followed by red hips. The foliage is lead-green. A rose of great historical significance, 'Alba Maxima' is sometimes known as the Great White, Jacobite or Cheshire rose, while others consider it to be the White Rose of York (see also 'Alba Semiplena').

■ LEFT

'ALBA SEMIPLENA'

Alba rose, known in gardens since at least the 16th century. It is a graceful shrub with a height of 2m (6ft) and a spread of 1.5m (5ft). In summer, clusters of semi-double, very fragrant, milky-white flowers open flat to display prominent golden stamens. Red hips form in late summer to autumn. 'Alba Semiplena' is usually held to be the White Rose of York (see also 'Alba Maxima').

■ LEFT

'CELESTE'

Alba rose with a lax and spreading habit that produces a shrub 2m (6ft) high and across, or more. The semi-double, sweetly scented, shell-pink flowers, with petals that appear almost transparent, are borne in summer and open flat to reveal prominent golden stamens. Red hips succeed them in autumn. The leaves are grey-green. The date of introduction of 'Céleste' is unrecorded, but it is certainly a very old cultivar. It is sometimes listed as 'Celestial'.

■ ABOVE

'FELICITE PARMENTIER'

Alba rose, known since about 1834, that grows into a compact shrub 1.2m (4ft) high and across. In mid-summer, it bears clusters of cup-shaped, highly scented, quartered, pale blush-pink flowers that open from primrose-yellow buds. The densely packed petals fade to almost white in hot sun and reflex to form a ball-shape. The leaves are grey-green. One of the daintiest of the albas, 'Félicité Parmentier' would suit the smallest garden.

■ ABOVE

'KONIGIN VON DANEMARK'

Alba rose, produced in 1826, that makes a tall, elegant bush up to 1.5m (5ft) high and 1.2m (4ft) across. The luminous pink flowers, borne in summer, are fully double, quartered rosette and richly scented, the colour fading to rose-pink as they mature. The leaves are pale greyish-green. 'Königin von Dänemark', sometimes sold as 'Queen of Denmark', has one of the longest flowering seasons – up to six weeks – and the flowers have good resistance to wet weather.

Bourbons

■ RIGHT

'LOUISE ODIER'

Bourbon rose, introduced in 1851, that makes a shrub 1.2m (4ft) high and across. From mid-summer to autumn, it produces cupped, fully double, strongly scented, lilac-tinted, warm-pink flowers. The leaves are light grey-green. 'Louise Odier' has slender shoots that can be supported on a pillar or tripod.

■ LEFT

'BOULE DE NEIGE'

Bourbon rose, introduced in 1867, growing to 1.5m (5ft) high and 1.2m (4ft) across, though the weight of the flowers may pull the slender stems further sideways; hence it is best with some support. In summer and autumn, clusters of red-tinted buds open to fully double, deeply cupped, strongly scented, white flowers. The leaves are leathery and dark green. 'Boule de Neige' (snowball) is so named because as the flowers develop the petals curl back to produce a ball shape.

■ RIGHT

'HONORINE DE BRABANT'

Bourbon rose, of unknown origin, that grows into a shrub about 2m (6ft) high and across. Its cupped, fully double, strongly but sweetly scented flowers are borne continuously from summer through to autumn, the autumn flowering being particularly good; the petals are pale pink, spotted and striped with mauve and crimson. The leaves are large and light green. 'Honorine de Brabant' tolerates poor soil; a sprawling rose, it is best with some support and may be trained as a short climber.

■ BELOW

'BLAIRII NUMBER TWO'

Bourbon rose, raised in 1845, that, if untrained, will grow into an arching shrub 2.1m (7ft) high and across or more. An abundance of large, cupped, fully double, sweetly scented flowers in mid-summer are pale silvery pink with deeper pink centres. The leaves, rough to the touch, are matt dark green. 'Blairii Number Two' produces few, if any, further blooms in autumn. Its vigour makes it suitable for growing as a pyramid, on a pergola or against a wall, where it can reach 5m (15ft).

■ LEFT

'SOUVENIR DE LA MALMAISON'

Bourbon rose, produced in 1843, growing into a dense shrub 1.5m (5ft) high and across. Repeating throughout summer, it bears very fragrant, fully double, soft pink flowers that open to a quartered-rosette shape as they fade to pinkish-white. The leaves are large. 'Souvenir de la Malmaison' is named in honour of Empress Josephine's famous garden at Malmaison; the silk-textured flowers may be spoilt by wet weather.

■ RIGHT

'MADAME ISAAC PEREIRE'

Bourbon rose, introduced in 1881, that grows into a large plant up to 2.1m (7ft) high and 2m (6ft) across. Borne from summer to autumn, the huge, richly fragrant, luminous deep cerise-pink flowers open as quartered rosettes but become muddled as they mature, especially those of the first flush. The matt dark green leaves are abundant. 'Madame Isaac Pereire', one of the most strongly scented of all roses, is a vigorous plant that can also be trained as a climber.

Centifolias and mosses

■ RIGHT

'CHAPEAU DE NAPOLEON'

Centifolia rose, bred in the 1820s. It is sometimes incorrectly included among the moss roses. It makes a graceful, slender-stemmed shrub 1.5m (5ft) high and 1.2m (4ft) across. In summer, it produces drooping, cupped, fully double, richly scented, deep silvery pink flowers that open flat and are sometimes quartered. The foliage is abundant. 'Chapeau de Napoléon' is now more correctly known as *R.* × *centifolia* 'Cristata'. The name 'Chapeau de Napoléon' refers to the unopened buds (see inset), which are three-cornered like the tricorn hat characteristically worn by Napoleon.

■ LEFT

'FANTIN-LATOUR'

Centifolia rose, dating from around 1900, that makes a handsome, vase-shaped shrub up to 2.1m (7ft) high and across. The flowers – cup-shaped, many-petalled, delicately scented and blush-pink – are borne in profusion over a long period in summer. The petals reflex to reveal a green button eye. The leaves are dark green. 'Fantin-Latour' was named in honour of the French flower painter Henri Fantin-Latour (1836–1904). Spraying against mildew may be necessary in summer.

■ LEFT

'NUITS DE YOUNG'

Moss rose, dating from 1845, that forms an upright then arching shrub 1.2m (4ft) high and 91cm (3ft) across. Small, double, lightly scented, maroon-purple flowers open flat in summer to reveal golden stamens. The leaves are small and dark green. 'Nuits de Young' is valued for its unique dusky colouring; even the mossing of the stems and buds is dark reddish-brown. Its other name, appropriately, is 'Old Black'.

■ RIGHT

'WILLIAM LOBB'

Moss rose, introduced in 1855, that makes an upright but sprawling shrub 2m (6ft) high and across. In mid-summer the large, double, rosette, heavily scented, magenta-purple flowers open from heavily mossed buds then fade to violet-grey. The dark green leaves are abundant. 'William Lobb' is a vigorous rose that benefits from some support; it can be trained as a short climber on a pillar or against a wall. The tonal range of the flowers as they mature and fade is remarkable.

Chinas and teas

■ RIGHT

'CECILE BRUNNER'

China rose, sometimes classified as a polyantha, introduced in 1880, that makes a dainty bush about 91cm (3ft) high and across. From summer to autumn, clusters of pointed buds open to urn-shaped, delicately scented, pale pink flowers that become more untidy as they age. The leaves are pointed and sparse. The buds are good for buttonholes, which may explain the common name, Sweetheart rose. Occasionally listed as 'Mignon', 'Cécile Brünner' is also sometimes known as the Maltese rose. A climbing form is available, and a rare white-flowered form.

■ LEFT

R. ODORATA 'MUTABILIS'

China rose, of uncertain parentage, introduced from China before 1894. It makes a dainty shrub about 91cm (3ft) high and across. The single, cupped, lightly scented flowers, borne through summer to autumn, are of unique colouring: flame orange in bud, they open to coppery yellow then fade to pink, deepening to purple as they age. The leaves are dark green and glossy. *R. odorata* 'Mutabilis' (sometimes sold as *R. chinensis* 'Mutabilis' or simply 'Mutabilis') appreciates a warm site against a wall; grown as a climber, it can reach a height of 2.4m (8ft) or more.

Damasks

■ RIGHT

'ISPAHAN'

Damask rose, first recorded in 1832 but probably much older; it may be Persian in origin. It makes a compact shrub with a height of 1.2–1.5m (4–5ft) and a spread of 91cm–1.2m (3–4ft). Large clusters of cupped, loosely double, reflexing, richly scented, clear pink flowers appear in summer. The grey-green foliage is attractive. 'Ispahan' has a longer flowering season than most other damasks and is in bloom for up to six weeks.

■ LEFT

'MADAME HARDY'

Damask rose, dating from 1867, that makes an elegant shrub up to 1.5m (5ft) high and across. Cupped, fully double, quartered-rosette, strongly scented white flowers are borne in profusion in summer, the petals reflexing to reveal a green button eye. The foliage is plentiful and matt light green. 'Madame Hardy' is generally considered to be one of the most sumptuous of old roses, though the flowers may be spoilt by rain.

Gallicas

■ RIGHT

'BELLE DE CRECY'

Gallica rose, bred before 1829, making a bush about 1.2m (4ft) high and 91cm (3ft) across. The quartered rosette, sweetly scented flowers, produced in abundance in mid-summer, open rich lilac-pink then fade to paler pink. The leaves are dull green. 'Belle de Crécy', though one of the best gallicas, has a laxer habit than most and its arching stems may require support.

■ LEFT

'CHARLES DE MILLS'

Gallica rose that makes a compact shrub up to 1.2m (4ft) in height with a spread of 91cm (3ft) or more. The fully double, quartered-rosette, moderately scented, rich crimson flowers, which are produced in summer, fade with grey and purple tones as they mature. The abundant foliage is matt dark green. 'Charles de Mills', sometimes sold as 'Bizarre Triomphant', has slender stems that may need staking to support the large flowers. Its parentage and date of introduction are unknown.

■ OPPOSITE

'CARDINAL DE RICHELIEU'

Gallica rose, produced in 1840, that makes a compact bush 1.2m (4ft) high and across, more if the stems are supported. In mid-summer it bears clusters of sumptuous, scented, dark maroon flowers, the petals of which are velvety in texture and reflex as the flowers age to form a ball shape. The stems are well covered with dark green leaves. 'Cardinal de Richelieu' needs good growing conditions and regular thinning of the old wood to give of its best. It can be used for hedging.

■ LEFT

'COMPLICATA'

Gallica rose that, as a free-standing shrub, grows to 2.4m (8ft) high and wide. The single, cupped, sweetly scented flowers, produced in abundance in summer, are bright porcelain-pink and open wide to reveal white centres and golden stamens. The leaves are matt greyish-green and, unusually for a gallica, rather pointed. 'Complicata' is not typical of its group and is of uncertain origin. It can be used as a rambler among trees and shrubs in a wild garden or can be trained on a pillar; it tolerates light, sandy soils.

■ LEFT

'DUCHESSE DE MONTEBELLO'

Gallica rose, bred before 1829, that makes a spreading bush about 1.2m (4ft) high and across. The open-cupped, fully double, sweetly fragrant flowers are soft blush-pink. The foliage is light green. 'Duchesse de Montebello' is one of the daintiest and neatest-growing of the gallicas.

■ ABOVE RIGHT

'DU MAITRE D'ECOLE'

Gallica rose that makes a compact plant about 91cm (3ft) high and across, wider in summer when the weight of blossom makes the stems arch over. The fully double, quartered-rosette, carmine-pink flowers open flat and fade to lilac-pink and grey. The dense, matt mid-green foliage is abundant. The date of introduction of 'Du Maître d'Ecole' is debated but is said by some authorities to be 1840.

■ RIGHT

'DUC DE GUICHE'

Gallica rose that forms a shrub 1.2m (4ft) high and across. In summer, it produces large, fully double, highly scented, rich crimson flowers; as they age, the petals develop purple veining, the flowers finally flushing purple. The leaves are matt dark green. 'Duc de Guiche', an outstanding gallica, is of uncertain origin and date.

■ RIGHT

R. GALLICA VAR. *OFFICINALIS*

Gallica rose, recorded in gardens since the 13th century. It makes a bushy shrub up to 1.2m (4ft) high and across. In summer, it produces an abundance of large, semi-double, sweetly fragrant, light crimson flowers that open flat to reveal golden stamens. The leaves are coarse. *R. gallica* var. *officinalis* is a superb garden plant that is rich in historical associations both as the Red Rose of Lancaster and the medieval apothecary's rose.

■ LEFT

'PRESIDENT DE SEZE'

Gallica rose, introduced before 1836, that grows into a sturdy shrub 1.2m (4ft) high by 91cm (3ft) across. In summer, it produces large, quartered, richly scented flowers; the centre petals are rich magenta-purple, the colour fading across the flower to soft lilac-pink, almost white, at the edges. The leaves are larger than is usual for a gallica. A well-grown specimen of 'Président de Sèze' is a remarkable sight when in full bloom.

■ LEFT

'TUSCANY SUPERB'

Gallica rose, raised before 1837, making an erect shrub 1.5m (5ft) high and 91cm (3ft) across. The large, semi-double, lightly scented, deep crimson flowers, produced in mid-summer, open flat, showing golden stamens, then fade to purple. The foliage is abundant. Tolerant of poor soil, 'Tuscany Superb' may be used for hedging; it richly deserves its other name, 'Double Velvet'.

■ LEFT

R. GALLICA 'VERSICOLOR'

Gallica rose, recorded in the 16th century but probably much older. It makes a neat shrub up to 1.2m (4ft) high and across. The lightly scented flowers, produced in mid-summer, are semi-double, opening flat to reveal golden stamens. The petals are pale pink, splashed and striped with red and crimson. The leaves are dull mid-green. *R. gallica* 'Versicolor' is commonly known as 'Rosa Mundi', after Fair Rosamund, the mistress of Henry II of England.

Other types

■ RIGHT

'BUFF BEAUTY'

Modern shrub rose, sometimes classified as a hybrid musk, bred probably before 1939. It grows to about 1.5m (5ft) high and across. The cupped, fully double, sweetly scented, pale buff-apricot flowers are carried in clusters in two flushes, the autumn flowering being less profuse. The leaves are tinged reddish-purple when young, turning dark green. 'Buff Beauty' can be used for hedging but, with the weight of the flowers on the canes, may need the support of horizontal wires. Mildew may be a problem in late summer.

■ LEFT

'CONSTANCE SPRY'

Modern shrub, sometimes classified as an 'English' rose, though it flowers once only, in summer. Introduced in 1961, untrained it makes a large, lax shrub up to 2m (6ft) high and across. The large, cupped, fully double, peony-like flowers are rich pink and heavily scented. The abundant leaves are dull green. 'Constance Spry' can also be grown as a climber on a pillar, or will tolerate shade against a wall. As a shrub it is best given some support or pruned hard to keep it compact.

■ RIGHT

'FRUHLINGSGOLD'

Scotch hybrid rose, sometimes classified as a modern shrub rose, introduced in 1937. It makes a vigorous shrub, each arching cane reaching up to 2.1m (7ft) long. The large, cupped, semi-double, fragrant, primrose-yellow flowers cover the canes in late spring to early summer. The flowers open flat from long, pointed buds to display golden stamens. The long green leaves are pointed. 'Frühlingsgold' is a tough, thorny plant that would be excellent planted as a barrier.

■ LEFT

'GRAHAM THOMAS'

Modern shrub or 'English' rose, raised in 1983, that forms a vigorous shrub 1.2m (4ft) high with a similar spread. The flowers, produced from summer to autumn, are cupped, fully double, fragrant and rich yellow. The leaves are glossy. Named in honour of the great English rosarian, Graham Stuart Thomas, 'Graham Thomas' was considered a notable introduction, since yellow is virtually absent among true old roses.

■ RIGHT

'GRUSS AN AACHEN'

Modern rose, usually classified as a cluster-flowered bush. It was bred around 1909 and makes a bush up to 91cm (3ft) high and across. The shapely, deeply cupped, fully double, delicately scented flowers are tinged pink on opening then fade to creamy white and are carried in clusters from summer to autumn. The leaves are dark green and leathery. Its long flowering season and low habit of growth make 'Gruss an Aachen' an outstanding bedding rose.

■ LEFT

'ROSERAIE DE L'HAY'

Rugosa rose, introduced in 1901, that makes a dense shrub up to 2.1m (7ft) high and across. The flowers are borne continuously through summer and into autumn. They are cupped (opening flat to reveal creamy stamens), fully double, heavily scented and rich wine-red. Few autumn hips are produced. The leaves are crinkled and bright green. 'Roseraie de l'Haÿ' is weather-resistant and makes a splendid hedge; since it tolerates poor soil and some shade, it can also be planted in light woodland.

■ ABOVE

'STANWELL PERPETUAL'

Scotch rose, raised in 1838, that forms a dense, prickly shrub that can reach 1.5m (5ft) high and across. The double, sweetly scented, blush-pink to white flowers that open flat are produced almost continuously throughout the summer. The leaves are grey-green. 'Stanwell Perpetual' tolerates poor soil and some shade, so may be planted in woodland; it also makes a good hedge.

MODERN ROSES

Most modern roses combine a cast-iron constitution with an unrivalled length of flowering. Some are dainty and elegant, others are richly coloured show-stoppers. Many are deliciously fragrant. In addition to their value in beds and borders, modern roses can be used in other parts of the garden. Their value as ground cover should not be overlooked, while those with a neat, compact habit are ideal for growing in a container, either on the terrace or a patio. There are even modern roses that have been bred to provide long-lasting blooms for the flower arranger.

■ PREVIOUS PAGE
'Alpine Sunset' has richly scented peach-pink flowers that shade to yellow.

■ RIGHT
Modern roses reward the gardener with beautiful flowers throughout summer.

The history of the modern rose

The history of the modern rose is usually held to have begun in 1867 with the introduction of 'La France'. Raised by Jean Guillot in France, it was considered an important novelty in rose breeding because it combined the long season and elegant flower shape of Chinese tea roses, from which it was descended, with the robust habit and hardiness of European roses.

'La France' was initially classified as a hybrid perpetual, a group of roses now more or less obsolete because they are leggy and difficult to place in the garden. It was soon realized, however, that this was a new type of rose, and the class hybrid tea was created. Today, hybrid teas are more correctly, if less elegantly, known as large-flowered bush roses.

■ LEFT
The radiant orange-red 'Top Marks' is a classic example of a dwarf cluster-flowered rose.

■ BELOW
One of the best yellow roses, 'Arthur Bell' shines out dramatically against a background of clipped yew.

Further selection and breeding refined the type, but the most significant breakthrough occurred early in the 20th century and involved the bright yellow *R. foetida* from central Asia (confusingly known as the Austrian briar). The species has two forms, 'Bicolor' (with vivid orange petals and a yellow reverse) and 'Persiana' (double flowers) that were also used, creating an unprecedented colour range

■ RIGHT
'White Pet', one of the first miniature roses, has stood the test of time.

including exciting bicolour and striped roses. The heyday of the old roses, with their somewhat restricted palette of white, pink and maroon, was over.

The new hybrid teas were bred with polyanthas – another largely obsolete rose group, which yields trusses of small flowers – to increase the flower size of the latter. The resulting roses were classified as hybrid polyanthas. Further breeding, notably in Britain, Denmark and the USA, produced roses with even larger flowers, though never as large as those of the hybrid tea.

'Rochester', introduced in 1934, was the first rose to be classified as a floribunda – producing smallish flowers in large sprays – but although the term was widely used, it never gained universal recognition. Other classifications included "floribunda hybrid-tea type" (for plants with large flowers) and "grandiflora" (for very tall roses), which meant that different terms were being used simultaneously for a range of roses that had certain broad similarities. Nowadays, all such roses are classified as cluster-flowered bush roses.

These two groups (the hybrid tea and floribunda) gradually came to dominate the rose market, being both easy to grow and reliable, and having a long flowering season. They proved ideal for bedding, and are still planted *en masse* for a bold display of solid blocks of colour in public parks and gardens. Towards the end of the 20th century, however, they lost some of their dominance with the revival of interest in cottage gardens in the style of the Edwardian garden designer Gertrude Jekyll. Old roses enjoyed a renaissance. Inevitably, breeders began looking for novelties to win back the attention of the gardening fraternity, and further hybridization produced several new classes. There are now roses for all manner of garden applications, including so-called patio roses, ground-cover roses, and miniatures. The recent trend towards dwarf, compact roses is remarkable. Miniature varieties first appeared early in the 19th century, but were regarded as little more than novelties for about 150 years. Today, with ever smaller gardens, their appeal has never been greater, and new varieties regularly appear to tempt the gardener (for further details of modern rose groups, see Classification and garden use).

Modern roses in the garden

■ BELOW LEFT
Two fine pink roses, 'Pink Parfait' with 'Queen Elizabeth' behind.

Such is the diversity of modern roses that their use in the garden is virtually unlimited. Whether you are looking for plants large or small, with strong or muted colours, rich perfume, a long flowering season, or for growing in containers, there is a rose to answer every need.

Bedding

For many gardeners, the large- and cluster-flowered roses are synonymous with bedding. A uniform effect is best created by sticking to one variety. If you want to mix varieties, check the final heights and group the tallest at the back of the border (or in the centre of an island bed), with shorter-growing varieties in front. By planting miniatures at their feet, you can create a bed that is roughly triangular in cross-section.

MODERN ROSES FOR BEDDING SCHEMES
'Alexander' (red)
'Allgold' (yellow)
'Chinatown' (golden-yellow)
'Elina' (ivory-white)
'Iceberg' (white)
'Just Joey' (orange)
'Sexy Rexy' (light rose-pink)
'Super Star' (vermilion)

For maximum impact, use the luminous 'Super Star', 'Precious Platinum' or 'Drummer Boy', which are among the best of the reds. 'Allgold' is a good yellow that keeps its colour well, while among the salmon-orange roses 'Anne Harkness' and 'Amber Queen' are outstanding. Possibly even more eye-catching are those that combine two colours, such as 'Piccadilly' (scarlet and yellow), 'Oranges and Lemons' (yellow, striped scarlet) and 'Circus' (whose flowers open yellow, mature to red,

■ RIGHT
Brilliant scarlet 'Fred Loads' sets alight a planting of herbaceous perennials.

and fade to orange, buff and pink). For more subtle schemes, 'Iceberg', 'Margaret Merril' and 'Pascali' are some of the most rain-resistant whites. It would be invidious to choose among the pinks, since there are so many excellent candidates, but 'Sexy Rexy' has a good clear colour, while 'Queen Elizabeth', a deeper cyclamen-pink, is one of the most versatile of all roses.

You can edge your rose bed with other bedding plants. Pelargoniums have a long flowering season and come in a similar colour range (though there is no yellow). Particularly useful are annuals such as African and French marigolds (*Tagetes*), which come in a cheery yellow or orange and attract beneficial insects that prey on aphids (see Pests, diseases and other disorders). If you wish to add a touch of blue, a colour which roses cannot offer, use ageratum or lobelia.

Standards

Standard roses are not trained as such, but are normal bush roses grafted on to stems of a vigorous species such as *Rosa rugosa* (see Propagation). They are available as full standards on a stem about 1.2m (4ft) high, or half-standards which are about 75cm (2½ft) high. They produce a lollipop shape, though grafted ground-cover roses (see Ground-cover roses) and climbers produce a weeping tree.

■ ABOVE
For added scent in the garden, you could try combining roses with annual tobacco *(Nicotiana)* plants.

You can deploy standards in a formal scheme to striking effect. They can rise above a sea of bedding roses, either to contrast with or complement them, or they can be used in a small garden to line a path, creating a kind of miniature, tree-lined avenue. Standards can also be used individually as eye-catchers to mark the end of a vista, or in a lawn, or in pairs to mark the start of a path or a flight of steps. To add style to a doorway, plant standards in pots, but when bare in winter they will need to be replaced by evergreen hollies (*Ilex*) or bays (*Laurus nobilis*).

■ LEFT
The cluster-flowered 'Eye Paint' planted *en masse* beneath *Gleditschia triacanthos* 'Sunburst'.

Roses as ground cover

Mostly of recent introduction and increasingly popular ground-cover roses generally have a compact, spreading habit, forming low, dome-shaped mounds. They look best in informal plantings.

Some are closely allied to rambling species that have a lax habit, and in some cases have inherited their single flowers. These suit a wild garden, combining well with other flowers that have not been heavily hybridized, such as poppies (*Papaver*) and species peonies, such as the excellent *Paeonia mlokosewitschii* (lemon yellow). 'Nozomi' (blush-white), one of the earliest of the type, is still one of the best for this purpose, but there are many more recent introductions that are equally suitable. 'Red Meidiland' (bright red) is outstanding, and has the advantage of conspicuous hips that redden in autumn.

Ground-cover roses can also be planted to cover banks or cascade over the sides of raised beds. They are equally effective in containers (see Planting a rose in a container) or rockeries. Mulch well in the garden, preferably with bark chippings, not because they are greedier than other types of rose but to help suppress any weeds. Unlike other ground-cover plants, they do not always form weed-suppressing mats, and weeding through the thorny stems can be a thankless task.

MODERN ROSES FOR HEDGING
'Alexander'
'Anne Harkness'
'Chinatown'
'Queen Elizabeth'
'Super Star'

Other uses

Some modern roses can be planted as hedges. While they have an unrivalled flowering season among hedging plants, they do have the disadvantage of being deciduous, and cannot provide a year-round barrier. Two fine varieties are 'Chinatown' (golden-yellow) and 'Queen Elizabeth' (pink), both of which reach 2m (6½ft) or more if lightly pruned (see Pruning). Other roses will form lower hedges, rugosas being especially effective with their tough, attractive foliage. Miniatures, such as 'Baby Masquerade', make an attractive low hedge or border edging in place of the traditional box or lavender.

Some modern roses also make highly effective lawn specimens. 'Chinatown' is a very good candidate, but 'Iceberg' is better still. Requiring only the minimum of pruning over a number of years, it will develop into an impressive shrub whose shape lives up to its name.

■ BELOW
A pair of weeping standards used to mark the entrance to a pathway.

Roses with other plants

Mixed planting is now in vogue, with all types of plant (shrubs, herbaceous perennials, bulbs and annuals) being grown together to make an informal scheme providing pleasure over a long season. Such a mix also attracts a wide range of beneficial insects. Roses are prime candidates for the mixed border, but note that they are best kept at a distance from other greedy shrubs and trees which may compete for moisture and nutrients (see Cultivation and planting).

Certain shrubs make dramatic backdrops. The dense, blackish-green of a yew hedge looks good with roses of any colouring, but more adventurous gardeners might prefer the grey-green *Eucalyptus gunnii* or, more dramatically, a purple-leaved form of *Berberis thunbergii* or *Cotinus coggygria*, sensational behind a vivid orange rose such as 'Whisky Mac'. Cut these shrubs back hard annually for the best foliage effect.

For an old world look, mix your roses with any of the traditional cottage-garden herbaceous plants. Lupins (*Lupinus*), Canterbury bells (*Campanula medium*) or foxgloves (*Digitalis*) will provide strong verticals, while frothy yellow-green lady's mantle (*Alchemilla mollis*) or bronze fennel (*Foeniculum vulgare* 'Purpureum') are marvellous fillers. Additionally, try the larger, striking alliums with their spherical heads of almost geometric precision. For a slightly more informal look in your garden, opt for Peruvian lilies (*Alstroemeria ligtu* hybrids) or day lilies (*Hemerocallis*), both of which now have an extended range of cultivars in a variety of colours.

Since modern roses flower for several months, you will need a few late-flowering accompanying perennials such as anemones,

■ RIGHT
This scheme combines a large-flowered rose with *Geum* 'Mrs Bradshaw', *Lychnis chalcedonica* and *Valeriana officinalis.*

crocosmias or cannas. Some tender perennials also have a comparably long flowering season, notably osteospermums and the blue *Felicia amelloides*. Half-hardy annuals such as tobacco plants (*Nicotiana*) also combine well with roses, as does the Texan bluebell (*Eustoma grandiflorum*). To maintain the display until the first frosts, make sowings throughout the spring. For a jungle-like effect, let a late-flowering clematis – a texensis or viticella type such as 'Gravetye Beauty' (crimson red) or 'Minuet' (white) – wander through neighbouring plants. Cut back hard annually when you prune the roses (see Pruning).

For a vibrant colour scheme, mix the rich amber-yellow 'Glenfiddich' or vermilion 'Alexander' with a red hot poker such as *Kniphofia* 'Prince Igor' (orange-red), and the aptly named *Crocosmia* 'Lucifer' (red). *Hemerocallis* 'Scarlet Orbit' could complete the picture, with annual orange nasturtiums at their feet. You can easily tone down this lively colour scheme with grey-leaved lambs' ears (*Stachys byzantina*), the grey curry plant (*Helichrysum italicum* subsp. *serotinum*) or one of the artemisias.

For an altogether gentler scheme, try the queen of foliage plants, the hosta. Roses with pink in their colouring look best with glaucous hostas such as *H. sieboldiana* 'Elegans' or 'Frances Williams', while the

■ BELOW
'Iceberg' planted *en masse* with pinks *(Dianthus)* and hardy geraniums.

■ RIGHT
'Amber Queen' planted to echo the shape of classical columns.

yellows and reds mix well with the brighter 'Sum and Substance' or 'August Moon'. Subtly coloured carnations and pinks (*Dianthus*) also blend well with roses, and have the advantage of attractive foliage.

There are many excellent modern roses for the scented garden. Create an even richer fragrance by stirring in the delicious *Lilium regale* and annual tobacco plants, Dame's violet (*Hesperis matronalis*), mignonette (*Reseda odorata*) and sweet peas (*Lathyrus odoratus*). A large mock orange (*Philadelphus*) will make a glorious scented backdrop.

Modern roses grown for their scent

'Alec's Red'	'Fragrant Cloud'
'Alexander'	'Helen Traubel'
'Apricot Nectar'	'Ingrid Bergman'
'Arthur Bell'	'Josephine Bruce'
'Betty Prior'	'Lady Hillingdon'
'Blue Moon	'Margaret Merril'
'Bobby Charlton'	'Mister Lincoln'
'Crimson Glory'	'Red Devil'
'Double Delight'	'Royal William'
'Dutch Gold'	'Sheila's Perfume'
'Elizabeth Harkness'	'Sutter's Gold'
'English Miss'	'Whisky Mac'
'Escapade'	'Yesterday'

Roses in containers

With the trend towards ever smaller gardens, rose breeders have turned towards dwarf, more compact roses that can be grown in containers. Some are no more than 30cm (1ft) high. You can grow them individually or make the rose the centrepiece of a large container, surrounding it with ivies (*Hedera*), trailing lobelia or the tender *Lotus berthelotii* (orange-red to scarlet) and *Helichrysum petiolare*. The tiniest roses can be planted in hanging baskets, some of the smaller ground-cover types with trailing stems being particularly effective.

Plant Directory

In the following section, roses are arranged according to the following categories: cluster-flowered, dwarf cluster-flowered and miniature, ground-cover, large-flowered and rugosa roses.

Heights and spreads are what the rose can be expected to achieve given good growing conditions. They may vary depending on climate, season and soil types.

Cluster-flowered roses

■ RIGHT

'AMBER QUEEN'

(syn. 'Harroony', 'Prinz Eugen van Savoyen')
Cluster-flowered rose, of neat habit, introduced in 1984. During summer and autumn, it produces clusters of fully double, heavily scented, rich amber-yellow flowers that open from rounded buds. The leaves are tinged red on emergence. Height and spread 50cm (20in). Good for bedding and hedges, 'Amber Queen' is also an outstanding choice for a container.

■ RIGHT

'APRICOT NECTAR'

Cluster-flowered rose, of bushy habit, introduced in 1965. From summer to autumn, it produces tight clusters of large, fully double, sweetly scented, pinkish buff-apricot flowers. The leaves are rounded. Height 80cm (32in), spread 65cm (26in). 'Apricot Nectar' is suitable for a hedge; mildew can be a problem in some areas.

■ RIGHT

'ANNE HARKNESS'

(syn. 'Harkaramel')
Cluster-flowered rose, of upright, branching habit, introduced in 1980. The pointed, urn-shaped, double, soft buff-yellow flowers are borne in large clusters from late summer to autumn. The leaves are mid-green. Height 1.2m (4ft), spread 60cm (2ft). Spectacular in full flower, 'Anne Harkness' is a disease-resistant rose that is suitable for bedding, hedging and cutting.

■ BELOW

'ARTHUR BELL'

Cluster-flowered rose, of upright, branching habit, introduced in 1965. From summer to autumn, it produces clusters of semi-double to double, strongly scented, bright yellow flowers that pale as they age. The leaves are leathery and glossy. Height to 90cm (3ft), spread 60cm (2ft). 'Arthur Bell' is a versatile rose, suitable for bedding, hedging and containers; the autumn flowering is especially good.

■ FAR LEFT

'CHINATOWN'

(syn. 'Ville de Chine')
Cluster-flowered rose, of bushy, upright habit, introduced in 1963. Clusters of fully double, fragrant, bright golden-yellow flowers are freely produced throughout the summer into autumn. The leaves are glossy dark green. Height 1.5m (5ft), spread 90cm (3ft). One of the largest of its type, 'Chinatown' can be grown at the back of a border, as a hedge or specimen.

■ ABOVE RIGHT

'ELIZABETH OF GLAMIS'

(syn. 'Irish Beauty')
Cluster-flowered rose, of upright habit, introduced in 1964. Clusters of double, sweetly scented, soft salmon-pink flowers are carried throughout the summer and autumn. The leaves are dark green and semi-glossy. Height 75cm (2½ft), spread 60cm (2ft). 'Elizabeth of Glamis' is an outstanding rose of its type and has stood the test of time; however, it does not always thrive on cold, heavy soils.

■ LEFT

'CIRCUS'

Cluster-flowered rose, of upright, branching habit, introduced in 1956. Throughout the summer, clusters of yellow buds open to shapely, cupped, fully double, slightly fragrant flowers with orange-yellow petals suffused with pink. The leaves are glossy dark green. Height 75cm (2½ft), spread 60cm (2ft). 'Circus', though of unique colouring, has lost some of its former popularity because of its susceptibility to disease.

■ ABOVE LEFT

'ESCAPADE'

(syn. 'Harpade')
Cluster-flowered rose, of freely branching habit, introduced in 1967. The semi-double, sweetly scented flowers are of unique colouring: borne in clusters from summer to autumn, they are soft lilac-pink, opening flat to reveal white centres and golden stamens. The leaves are glossy bright green. Height to 1.2m (4ft), spread 60cm (2ft). A disease-resistant rose, 'Escapade' is good for cutting and in mixed plantings; it occasionally produces pure white flowers within the cluster.

■ ABOVE RIGHT

'HANNAH GORDON'

(syn. 'Korweiso', 'Raspberry Ice')
Cluster-flowered rose, of spreading, open habit, introduced in 1983. In summer and autumn, it produces clusters of lightly scented, double flowers that have creamy pink petals shading to deeper pink at the edges. The leaves are glossy dark green. Height 80cm (32in), spread 65cm (26in). 'Hannah Gordon', a disease-resistant rose, is good for cutting and can also be grown in a container.

■ LEFT

'EYE PAINT'

(syn. 'Maceye', 'Tapis Persan')
Cluster-flowered rose, of bushy, free-branching habit, introduced in 1975. Large clusters of single, lightly scented flowers cover the bush during summer and autumn; bright scarlet, they open flat to reveal white centres and golden stamens. Height to 1.2m (4ft), spread 75cm (2½ft). 'Eye Paint' does best with light pruning and makes a good hedge; deadhead regularly to maintain the flowering performance.

■ RIGHT

'ICEBERG'

(syn. 'Fée des Neiges', 'Korbin', 'Schneewittchen')
Cluster-flowered rose, of elegant, branching habit, introduced in 1958. From summer to autumn, clusters of double, ivory-white, lightly scented flowers, carried in abundance, open from tapering, pink-flushed buds. The leaves are glossy bright green. Height to 1.5m (5ft), spread to 90cm (3ft) or more. An outstanding rose of its type, 'Iceberg' can be used for bedding, hedging, cutting or, with minimum pruning, as a specimen.

■ LEFT

'KORRESIA'

(syn. 'Friesia', 'Sunsprite')
Cluster-flowered rose, of neat, upright habit, introduced in 1974. From summer to autumn, clusters of shapely buds open to double, fragrant, bright golden-yellow flowers that hold their colour well. The leaves are glossy light green. Height 75cm (2½ft), spread 60cm (2ft). 'Korresia' can be used for bedding and to provide cut flowers; it is similar to 'Allgold' but has bigger flowers.

■ ABOVE LEFT

'LILLI MARLENE'

Cluster-flowered rose, of slender, branching habit, introduced in 1959. Large clusters of double, only lightly scented, deep rich crimson flowers are produced from summer to autumn on plum-red shoots. The leaves are glossy dark green, tinted red on emergence. Height 70cm (28in), spread 60cm (2ft). 'Lilli Marlene' is tolerant of both rain and hot sun, and makes a good hedge.

■ ABOVE RIGHT

'MASQUERADE'

Cluster-flowered rose, of compact habit, introduced in 1949. From summer to autumn, clusters of yellow buds open to semi-double, only lightly scented, salmon-pink flowers that age to deep red, with all colours present simultaneously. The leaves are glossy dark green. Height 90cm (3ft), spread 75cm (2½ft). 'Masquerade' makes an excellent hedge; deadhead regularly to maintain flowering.

■ ABOVE

'MARGARET MERRIL'

(syn. 'Harkuly')

Cluster-flowered rose, of upright habit, introduced in 1977. Clusters of large, shapely, double, sweetly scented, pure white flowers are carried from summer to autumn. The leaves are glossy dark green. Height 90cm (3ft), spread 60cm (2ft). Besides its versatility in the garden, 'Margaret Merril' can also be grown in containers and used as a cut flower, but blackspot can be a problem.

■ ABOVE LEFT

'MOUNTBATTEN'

(syn. 'Harmantelle')
Cluster-flowered rose, of dense, upright habit, introduced in 1982. Small clusters of large, double, lightly scented, mimosa-yellow flowers are carried from summer to autumn. The leaves are glossy dark green. Height to 1.5m (5ft), spread to 90cm (3ft). A vigorous rose that, with minimum pruning, makes an excellent specimen.

■ ABOVE RIGHT

'QUEEN ELIZABETH'

(syn. 'The Queen Elizabeth Rose')
Cluster-flowered rose, of strongly upright habit, introduced in 1954. From summer to autumn, it produces clusters of large, fully double, only lightly scented, deep china-pink flowers. The leaves are glossy dark green. Height to 2m (6½ft) or more, spread 90cm (3ft). 'Queen Elizabeth' is an outstanding rose but can be difficult to place in the garden: use it at the back of a border or as a hedge. The flowers last well when cut.

■ LEFT

'SEXY REXY'

(syn. 'Heckenzauber', 'Macrexy')
Cluster-flowered rose, of upright habit, introduced in 1984. Clusters of shapely, fully double, lightly scented, clear light pink flowers are produced in summer and autumn. The leaves are glossy dark green. Height and spread 60cm (2ft). A versatile rose, 'Sexy Rexy' is good for garden use, in containers, and as a cut flower.

■ ABOVE

'SHEILA'S PERFUME'

(syn. 'Harsherry')
Cluster-flowered rose, of upright habit, introduced in 1985. The flowers, carried singly and in clusters from summer to autumn, are double and sweetly scented; the petals are yellow marked with red, fading to pink. The leaves are glossy dark green. Height 75cm (2½ft), spread 60cm (2ft). 'Sheila's Perfume' makes an excellent low hedge, grows well in containers, and provides good cut flowers.

■ ABOVE RIGHT

'THE FAIRY'

Cluster-flowered rose, usually classified as a polyantha, of dense, mounding habit, introduced in 1932. From late summer to late autumn, clusters of small, double, virtually scentless, light pink flowers appear in profusion. The leaves are glossy mid-green. Height and spread 60cm (2ft) or more. A dainty rose, 'The Fairy' is valued principally for its late flowering season.

■ LEFT

'YESTERDAY'

(syn. 'Tapis d'Orient')
Cluster-flowered rose, usually classified as a polyantha, of elegant, open, spreading habit, introduced in 1974. From summer to autumn, clusters of semi-double, fragrant, deep lilac-pink flowers, produced in succession, open flat to reveal paler centres and golden stamens. The leaves are glossy dark green. Height and spread 90cm (3ft) or more. 'Yesterday' has any number of uses in the garden and provides good cut flowers; with light pruning, it makes an attractive specimen.

Dwarf cluster-flowered and miniature roses

■ ABOVE LEFT

'ANNA FORD'

(syn. 'Harpiccolo')
Dwarf cluster-flowered rose, of dense, low, free-branching habit, introduced in 1981. The warm orange-red flowers, produced freely from summer to autumn, open flat from pointed buds to reveal yellow centres. The leaves are glossy dark green. Height 45cm (1½ft), spread 38cm (15in). 'Anna Ford' was one of the first of its type and is still popular as a bedding or container rose.

■ ABOVE RIGHT

'BABY MASQUERADE'

(syn. 'Baby Carnival', 'Tanba', 'Tanbakede')
Miniature rose, of upright, bushy habit, introduced in 1956. From summer to autumn, it carries clusters of tiny, double flowers that open yellow and fade to pink, then deeper red. The plentiful leaves are dark green. Height and spread 40cm (16in). A healthy rose, 'Baby Masquerade' can be used for bedding; it is widely available as a standard.

■ LEFT

'CINDERELLA'

Miniature rose, of upright, bushy habit, introduced in 1952. Clusters of fully double, only lightly scented, blush-pink flowers are produced in abundance from summer to autumn. The tiny leaves are pointed and glossy. Height and spread to 25cm (10in). An outstanding miniature, 'Cinderella' is virtually unique of its type because it is best with some shade.

■ RIGHT

'QUEEN MOTHER'

(syn. 'Korquemu')
Dwarf cluster-flowered rose, of spreading habit, introduced in 1991. The semi-double, only lightly scented, clear pink flowers are produced from summer to autumn. The leaves are small and glossy. Height 45cm (1½ft), spread 60cm (2ft). 'Queen Mother' can be used as ground cover and is excellent in a container; it is sometimes available as a weeping standard.

■ ABOVE LEFT

'RISE 'N' SHINE'

(syn. 'Golden Meillandina', 'Golden Sunblaze')
Miniature rose, of upright, branching habit, introduced in 1977. From summer to autumn, clusters of fully double, virtually scentless, deep yellow flowers are borne. The leaves are small and pointed. Height 45cm (1½ft), spread 40cm (16in). 'Rise 'n' Shine' is one of the best miniature yellow roses and is good for cutting.

■ ABOVE RIGHT

'SWEET DREAM'

(syn. 'Fryminicot')
Dwarf cluster-flowered rose, of stiffly upright habit, introduced in 1988. From summer to autumn, it produces an abundance of fully double, lightly scented, soft apricot-orange flowers. The leaves are matt dark green. Height 40cm (16in), spread 35cm (14in). An outstanding rose of its type, 'Sweet Dream' can be used for low hedging or to edge a border.

Ground-cover roses

■ LEFT

'AVON'

(syn. 'Fairy Lights', 'Poulmulti', 'Sunnyside') Ground-cover rose, of low, compact, spreading habit, introduced in 1992. From summer to autumn, clusters of small, semi-double, fragrant, pinkish-white flowers open flat to reveal golden stamens. The leaves are glossy mid-green. Height 30cm (1ft), spread 90cm (3ft). Besides making excellent ground cover, 'Avon' can also be grown successfully in containers.

■ RIGHT

'WHITE FLOWER CARPET'

(syn. 'Heidetraum', 'Noatraum') Ground-cover rose, of spreading habit, introduced in 1991. From summer to autumn, and sometimes later, it produces clusters of small, double, only lightly scented, pure white flowers. The leaves are glossy. Height 75cm (2½ft), spread 1.2m (4ft). Aptly named, 'White Flower Carpet' can be used to cover a bank, or grown in containers.

Large-flowered roses

■ ABOVE

'ALEXANDER'

(syn. 'Alexandra')
Large-flowered rose, of upright habit, introduced in 1972. The double, luminous red flowers open from pointed buds from summer to autumn. The leaves are glossy dark green. Height to 2m (6½ft), spread 75cm (2½ft). 'Alexander', a disease-resistant rose, bears its flowers on long stems that make them particularly suitable for cutting.

■ ABOVE

'ALEC'S RED'

(syn. 'Cored')
Large-flowered rose, of bushy habit, introduced in 1970. Large, fully double, heavily scented, rich red flowers open from pointed buds throughout summer and into autumn. The leaves are dark green. Height 90cm (3ft), spread 60cm (2ft). 'Alec's Red' is a versatile rose, suitable for cutting, bedding, and as a hedge.

■ RIGHT

'BIG PURPLE'

(syn. 'Nuit d'Orient', 'Stebigpu', 'Stephens' Big Purple')
Large-flowered rose, of upright habit, introduced in 1987. The large, rich purplish-red flowers are fully double and heavily scented, appearing from summer to autumn. The leaves are dark green. Height 90cm (3ft), spread 60cm (2ft). 'Big Purple', of almost unique colouring, is good for bedding and cutting.

■ ABOVE LEFT

'BLUE MOON'

(syn. 'Blue Monday', 'Mainzer Fastnacht', 'Sissi', 'Tannacht')
Large-flowered rose, of upright, branching habit, introduced in 1964. In summer and autumn, shapely, fully double, silvery lilac flowers that are sweetly scented are carried in abundance. The leaves are large and dark green. Height 90cm (3ft), spread 60cm (2ft). Generally considered to be the best "blue" rose, 'Blue Moon' needs careful placing in the garden because of its curious colouring; it is perhaps best grown under glass.

■ ABOVE RIGHT

'BOBBY CHARLTON'

Large-flowered rose, of upright habit, introduced in 1974. It produces high-centred, fully double, scented, soft pink flowers from late summer to autumn. The large leaves are dark green and semi-glossy. Height 90cm (3ft), spread 60cm (2ft). Generally a healthy rose, 'Bobby Charlton' performs well in wet weather and is a good choice for exhibition.

■ RIGHT

'CHRYSLER IMPERIAL'

Large-flowered rose, of neat, upright habit, introduced in 1952. The very fragrant, fully double, vivid red flowers open from pointed buds then fade to dull purplish-red. The leaves are dark green. Height 90cm (3ft), spread 60cm (2ft). 'Chrysler Imperial' is grown exclusively for the perfection of individual flowers and is a good rose for exhibition if disbudded; its propensity to disease makes it a poor choice for other purposes.

■ BELOW RIGHT

'DOUBLE DELIGHT'

(syn. 'Andeli')
Large-flowered rose, of freely branching habit, introduced in 1977. From summer to autumn, it produces large, shapely, fully double, sweetly scented flowers that have creamy-white petals flushed cherry-red at the edges. The leaves are semi-glossy. Height 90cm (3ft), spread 60cm (2ft). 'Double Delight' is an outstanding rose that is good for bedding and cutting, though the flowers can be spoilt by rain.

■ OPPOSITE BELOW

'CHICAGO PEACE'

Large-flowered rose, of bushy, spreading habit, introduced in 1962. The huge, only lightly scented flowers, produced from summer to autumn, have coppery pink petals with a yellow reverse. The leaves are glossy dark green. Height to 1.5m (5ft), spread 90cm (3ft). 'Chicago Peace', a sport (spontaneous mutation) of 'Peace', can be used as a specimen if pruned only lightly; otherwise, use it for bedding or hedging.

■ ABOVE LEFT

'DUTCH GOLD'

Large-flowered rose, of upright habit, introduced in 1978. The shapely, fully double, bright golden-yellow flowers, carried from summer to autumn, are sweetly scented. The leaves are glossy dark green. Height 90cm (3ft), spread 60cm (2ft). 'Dutch Gold' is an excellent bedding rose; the flowers hold their colour well.

■ ABOVE RIGHT

'ELINA'

(syn. 'Dicjana', 'Peaudouce')
Large-flowered rose, of bushy habit, introduced in 1985. During summer and autumn, fully double, lightly scented, creamy white flowers open to reveal lemon-yellow flushed centres. The leaves are tinted red. Height 90cm (3ft), spread 75cm (2½ft). 'Elina' is a versatile rose that is easy to grow; generally healthy, it can be used for bedding and cutting.

■ LEFT

'ELIZABETH HARKNESS'

Large-flowered rose, of upright habit, introduced in 1969. From summer to autumn, it produces shapely, fully double, fragrant, ivory-white flowers that flush pink as they age. The leaves are semi-glossy. Height 75cm (2½ft), spread 60cm (2ft). 'Elizabeth Harkness' is good for cutting and bedding; the flowers are of perfect form but can be spoilt by wet weather.

■ LEFT

'FRAGRANT CLOUD'

(syn. 'Duftwolke', 'Nuage Parfum', 'Tanellis')
Large-flowered rose, of sturdy, branching habit, introduced in 1963. The large, fully double, richly scented, bright geranium-red flowers, ageing to purplish-red, are carried from summer to autumn. The leaves are leathery and dark green. Height 75cm (2½ft), spread 60cm (2ft). 'Fragrant Cloud' is an outstanding rose that can be used for bedding or cutting; the fragrance is virtually unsurpassed among modern roses.

■ RIGHT

'GRANDPA DICKSON'

(syn. 'Irish Gold')
Large-flowered rose, of very upright habit, introduced in 1966. Large, double, only lightly scented flowers, freely borne from summer to autumn, are soft pale yellow, occasionally flushed with pink. The leaves are small and light green. Height 75cm (2½ft), spread 60cm (2ft). Its disease resistance and tolerance of rough weather make 'Grandpa Dickson' an outstanding bedding rose; for top quality performance good cultivation is essential.

■ ABOVE LEFT

'INGRID BERGMAN'

(syn. 'Poulman')
Large-flowered rose, of upright, branching habit, introduced in 1984. The fully double, only lightly scented, deep red flowers are carried from summer to autumn. The leaves are glossy dark green. Height 75cm (2½ft), spread 60cm (2ft). Good for cutting, bedding and containers, 'Ingrid Bergman' is one of the best in its colour range.

■ ABOVE RIGHT

'JULIA'S ROSE'

Large-flowered rose, of upright but spindly habit, introduced in 1976. The shapely, double, urn-shaped flowers, produced from summer to autumn, are of unique colouring: the petals are coppery bronze to buff, shaded brownish-pink. The leaves are reddish-green and sparse. Height 75cm (2½ft), spread 45cm (1½ft). Despite its weak growth, 'Julia's Rose' is worth growing for the beauty of the individual flowers.

■ RIGHT

'KING'S RANSOM'

Large-flowered rose, of branching habit, introduced in 1961. From summer to autumn, it bears a profusion of fully double, lightly scented, pure yellow flowers. The leaves are glossy dark green. Height 75cm (2½ft), spread 60cm (2ft). 'King's Ransom' is excellent for bedding and as a cut flower, but does not do well on light, chalky (alkaline) soils.

■ RIGHT

'MISTER LINCOLN'

Large-flowered rose, of upright habit, introduced in 1964. Fully double, very fragrant, deep dusky-red flowers are produced in summer and autumn.
The leaves are matt dark green. Height to 1.2m (4ft), spread to 90cm (3ft). 'Mister Lincoln' is excellent for cutting, but tends to produce its flowers in clusters; disbud for prime quality blooms.

■ OPPOSITE BELOW

'JUST JOEY'

Large-flowered rose, of upright, branching habit, introduced in 1973. Elegant, long, shapely buds open to lightly scented, fully double, coppery orange-pink flowers with slightly ruffled petals. The matt dark green leaves are tinted red on emergence. Height 75cm (2½ft), spread 60cm (2ft). 'Just Joey' is an outstanding rose, valued for its freedom of flowering, general disease-resistance and versatility in the garden, besides the unusual colour of the blooms.

■ RIGHT

'OLYMPIAD'

(syn. 'Macauck')
Large-flowered rose, of upright, bushy habit, introduced in 1984. The fully double, only lightly scented, bright red flowers are produced from summer to autumn. The leaves are matt mid-green. Height 1.2m (4ft), spread 60cm (2ft). 'Olympiad' is an excellent rose for cutting.

■ BELOW LEFT

'PAPA MEILLAND'

(syn. 'Meisar')
Large-flowered rose, of upright habit, introduced in 1963. From summer to autumn, it produces shapely, fully double, strongly fragrant, deep crimson flowers. The leaves are glossy dark green. Height 90cm (3ft), spread 60cm (2ft). Excellent as a cut flower, 'Papa Meilland' is grown for the beauty of the individual blooms; on the debit side, flowering is not profuse, and the plant is prone to disease.

■ BELOW RIGHT

'PASCALI'

Large-flowered rose, of upright, open habit, introduced in 1963. Throughout summer and autumn, it produces shapely, double, only lightly scented flowers that have white petals shaded creamy buff. The leaves are glossy dark green, but sparse. Height 90cm (3ft), spread 75cm (2½ft). The flowers of 'Pascali' show unsurpassed rain-resistance; they are exceptionally long-lasting when cut.

■ RIGHT
‘PAUL SHIRVILLE’

(syn. ‘Harqueterwife’, ‘Heart Throb’) Large-flowered rose, of slightly spreading habit, introduced in 1983. The double, fragrant, warm pink flowers are carried from summer to autumn. The leaves are large and dark green. Height 90cm (3ft), spread 75cm (2½ft). ‘Paul Shirville’ tolerates poor soil and is good for bedding and containers.

■ LEFT
‘PEACE’

(syn. ‘Gioia’, ‘Gloria Dei’, ‘Mme A. Meilland’)
Large-flowered rose, of spreading, bushy habit, bred in 1942. The large, fully double, only lightly scented flowers are pale yellow with pink flushes, and appear from mid-summer to autumn. The leaves are glossy dark green. Height to 1.5m (5ft) or more, spread 90cm (3ft) or more. One of the most popular and best-known roses ever bred, ‘Peace’ is a vigorous plant that makes a fine specimen with light pruning.

■ OPPOSITE TOP

'ROYAL WILLIAM'

(syn. 'Duftzauber '84', 'Fragrant Charm '84', 'Korzaun')
Large-flowered rose, of upright habit, introduced in 1984. From summer to autumn, it carries large, fully double, fragrant, deep crimson flowers on long stems. The leaves are glossy dark green. Height 90cm (3ft), spread 75cm (2½ft). 'Royal William' is good for bedding and excellent for cutting.

■ BELOW

'RED DEVIL'

(syn. 'Coeur d'Amour')
Large-flowered rose, of bushy habit, introduced in 1967. From summer to autumn, it produces large, shapely, fully double, fragrant, vivid scarlet flowers. The leaves are glossy dark green. Height 90cm (3ft), spread 75cm (2½ft). 'Red Devil' is splendid for exhibition; it is also a good bedding rose, though the flowers can be spoilt by rain.

■ ABOVE

'PICCADILLY'

Large-flowered rose, of upright, branching habit, introduced in 1959. From summer to autumn, it produces double, only lightly scented flowers with bright scarlet petals with a yellow reverse ageing to orange. The leaves are glossy dark green, tinged bronze. Height 90cm (3ft), spread 60cm (2ft). 'Piccadilly' performs best in cool weather, bright sunlight turning the colour a more uniform orange; blackspot can be a problem.

■ BELOW LEFT

'SAVOY HOTEL'

(syn. 'Harvintage', 'Integrity')
Large-flowered rose, of bushy habit, introduced in 1989. From summer to autumn, strong stems carry large, shapely, fully double, fragrant, light clear pink flowers. The leaves are dark green. Height 90cm (3ft), spread 60cm (2ft). 'Savoy Hotel' is a versatile rose that provides excellent material for cutting; it needs good cultivation for top-rate performance.

■ BELOW RIGHT

'SUPER STAR'

(syn. 'Tanorstar', 'Tropicana')
Large-flowered rose, of branching but uneven habit, introduced in 1960. The large, shapely, double, lightly scented, luminous vermilion flowers are produced from summer to autumn. The leaves are semi-glossy. Height and spread 90cm (3ft). 'Super Star' is grown for the beauty of individual blooms and is difficult to place in a mixed border; it can be susceptible to mildew.

■ LEFT

'TROIKA'

(syn. 'Royal Dane')
Large-flowered rose, of upright, branching habit, introduced in 1972. From summer to autumn, it produces large, shapely, double, lightly scented, copper-orange flowers that are sometimes veined scarlet. The leaves are glossy dark green. Height 90cm (3ft), spread 75cm (2½ft). Disease- and weather-resistant, 'Troika' is a good choice for a massed planting and provides good cut flowers.

■ RIGHT

'WHISKY MAC'

(syn. 'Tanky', 'Whisky')
Large-flowered rose, of upright, bushy habit, introduced in 1967. From summer to autumn, it produces an abundance of large, fully double, strongly fragrant, rich amber-yellow flowers. The leaves are glossy dark green. Height 75cm (2½ft), spread 60cm (2ft). Despite sometimes suffering from dieback and fungal diseases, 'Whisky Mac' retains its popularity because of its unique flower colour.

Rugosa roses

■ RIGHT
'HANSA'

Rugosa rose, of dense habit, introduced in 1905. Double, very fragrant, reddish-purple flowers are freely produced throughout the summer; in autumn, large red hips develop. The leaves are tough, wrinkled and dark green. Height 1.2m (4ft), spread 90cm (3ft). A versatile rose, 'Hansa' can be grown as a specimen, in light shade, or as a hedge.

■ ABOVE
'ROSERAIE DE L'HAY'

Rugosa rose, of dense, spreading habit, introduced in 1901. Throughout the summer and into autumn, it produces double, strongly scented, wine-red flowers that open to reveal creamy stamens. The wrinkled leaves redden in autumn. Height 2m (6½ft) or more, spread 1.2m (4ft) or more. 'Roseraie de l'Hay' makes an excellent hedge and can also be planted in light shade.

■ ABOVE
'SCHNEEZWERG'

(syn. 'Snow Dwarf')
Rugosa rose, of dense, spreading habit, introduced in 1912. From late spring until late autumn, it produces anemone-like, semi-double, only lightly scented, white flowers that open flat to reveal golden stamens; small orange-red hips follow. The leaves are greyish-green. Height 1.2m (4ft), spread 1.5m (5ft). The autumn display of 'Schneezwerg' is particularly good, though the foliage does not change colour; flowers continue to appear alongside the reddening hips. For the best fruiting, deadhead selectively in summer.

CLIMBING ROSES

Few sights in the garden can compare with that of a climbing rose at the height of its glory. Each year at around summer's peak – and sometimes again later – the climbing roses put on a breath-taking display that is unmatched by any other group of plants. Many scent the air for some distance around them.

Climbing roses are multi-talented. They can embrace a conifer or an ancient oak tree, cover a wall or be trained to twine around a pergola to create a bower of flowers. They are also excellent for blocking or hiding unwanted views, such as an ugly shed or garage. Modern climbers come in a wide range of sizes and colours, and some can be grown in containers and enjoyed in the smallest garden.

■ PREVIOUS PAGE
A trellis is almost hidden by the masses of pink flowers of a rose in perfect health.

■ RIGHT
The rambling rose 'Seagull' frames a vista at the height of summer.

The history of climbing roses

Climbing roses are a disparate group of plants that share no common ancestor. The term "climbing rose" is usually understood to include rambling roses (often with large trusses of small flowers produced in a single flush in mid-summer) as well as true climbing roses that tend to flower recurrently. Ramblers generally produce masses of very flexible canes and flower on year-old wood; climbers, often more stiffly upright, flower on new wood (for details see Growth habits and flower shapes).

In the wild, few roses are natural climbers, but there are several that make huge, scrambling shrubs with long, flexible stems that are described botanically as scandent (ascending or loosely climbing). Such roses rapidly colonize any shrub or tree that impedes their progress by attaching themselves to the host plants by means of their sharp, hooked thorns.

Many climbing roses grown in gardens today have the Chinese species *Rosa gigantea* in their ancestry. As its name suggests, this is an enormous plant that can reach a height and spread of 16.5m (54ft) or more. Fortunately, most modern climbing roses are more restrained. Many rambling roses have been derived from *R. wichurana*, a species found in Japan, Korea, China and Taiwan, that has lax stems that either trail or climb. The evergreen European *R. sempervirens* has also played a part, as has the Japanese *R. multiflora*. *R. luciae*, similar to *R. wichurana*, has played a minor role.

Some climbing roses are sports (spontaneous mutations) of bush roses. A climbing sport can be recognized by having "Climbing" in its name, for example, 'Climbing Peace', 'Climbing Blue Moon' and 'Climbing Queen Elizabeth'.

■ OPPOSITE
The rambling rose 'Bleu Magenta' bears its flowers in clusters, as does one of its parents, the vigorous *R. multiflora.*

■ BELOW
An archetypal cottage garden rose, 'Zéphirine Drouhin' has the advantage of thornless stems.

Some of the old-fashioned Bourbon roses, such as 'Louise Odier' and 'Madame Isaac Pereire', both of which have long, flexible stems, can also be grown as climbers, as can some of the China roses.

Although roses have been popular garden plants for centuries, interest in the breeding of new varieties of climbing rose declined between the two World Wars. This lack of popularity was possibly due to the climbing rose's need for regular maintenance and the fact that many flowered only once. (A neglected climber can become a menace, making impenetrable thickets of tough, thorny stems.) As a result, with a few exceptions, most of the climbing roses grown in gardens today were bred after 1949. The two rose breeders who did most to revive interest in breeding climbing roses were Sam McGredy in Great Britain

■ OPPOSITE
The magnificent 'Climbing Iceberg' is a good choice for clothing a wall, where its flowers look most graceful.

■ BELOW
'Albertine', one of the best-loved rambling roses of all time, at the height of its glory in mid-summer.

and Wilhelm Kordes in Germany. Both concentrated on shorter growing varieties that were easier to manage. Breeders in the USA also made an important contribution, especially Dr Walter Van Fleet, who developed roses that could survive a cold North American winter. He bred the pink climber that bears his name, although today its repeat-flowering sport, 'New Dawn', has superseded it.

More recently, a number of "miniature" climbers have been introduced. These have small flowers and grow no more than 2.1m (7ft). They are ideal for the smaller garden or for growing in containers.

Climbing roses in the garden

■ BELOW
The richly scented shrub rose 'Constance Spry' can be trained against a wall, and tolerates some shade.

There are few more idyllic images than that of a country cottage in high summer, with roses arching over the gate and covering the walls of the house. Town-dwellers can recreate this effect too. A climbing rose will lend an air of timelessness and maturity, even to the most modern home. Choose one of the heavily scented varieties, such as 'Albertine', 'New Dawn' or 'Zéphirine Drouhin'. Their scent will be especially appreciated near an open window. 'Zéphirine Drouhin' is particularly well suited for growing around a door because it has no thorns to catch on the clothing of passers-by.

Climbing roses have a number of other uses in the garden. Where there is space, you could allow the rose to grow with the minimum of pruning

■ BELOW
A climbing rose trained along a rope in a catenary or curve looks delightful.

■ BELOW
Clematis 'The President' makes a sensational clash with the brilliant scarlet climbing rose 'Danse du Feu'.

to produce a huge fountain of flowers. The rambling 'Albertine', grown in this way, makes a magnificent 6m (20ft) high shrub, and is one of the glories of the mid-summer garden.

'Albertine' and some other ramblers are available as weeping standards, grafted on to 1.2–1.8m (4–6ft) stems of *R. canina* or *R. rugosa*, so that you can create a cascade of flowers even in a confined area.

Climbing roses also look stunning grown over pergolas. Rustic poles are appropriate in cottage gardens, although brick pillars linked by wooden beams may last longer.

You can also train roses on ropes slung between two uprights to create garlands of flowers, called a catenary, at the back of a border. For this purpose, choose a medium-growing variety with long, flexible stems, such as 'Madame Grégoire Staechelin' that can be looped around the rope to produce festoons of flowers. Shorter-growing types, such as 'Golden Showers' or 'Handel', or one of the Bourbon roses, such as 'Madame Isaac Pereire' or 'Louise Odier', can be planted in the border and trained against pillars or tripods. Another possibility is to erect free-standing trellis panels. Train the roses against these to make a barrier that will be covered in flowers in summer but open in winter.

Rampant roses that grow up to and over 12m (40ft) high are best accommodated in most gardens by allowing them to scramble through trees, but take care to choose a

■ LEFT
A climbing or rambling rose can make a spectacular impression if grown up a tree.

■ BELOW
The banana-scented 'Seagull' wings its way through a large mature conifer.

suitably robust host plant that will be able to take the weight of the fully grown rose. Large conifers planted principally for winter interest are good candidates. An old orchard of apple or cherry trees would look enchanting wreathed in climbing roses that form great crinolines of flowers about the branches. Although this is a spectacular way of growing roses such as 'Climbing Cécile Brünner', 'Seagull' or 'Albéric Barbier', bear in mind that the vigour of the rose must be matched to the size of the tree. A large vigorous rambler will very soon smother a small tree, eventually leading to its demise.

Climbing roses can also be grown informally, but effectively, by allowing them to ramble through shrubs, such as lilacs, which are dull after their show of flowers in late spring. This is a form of wild gardening, since a strict pruning regime in such a situation would be impractical.

You can trail a climbing rose up and over a wall to make a curtain of flowers on the other side. If you have a high garden wall, try pinning to it one of the more vigorous climbing roses, such as 'Paul's Lemon Pillar'. If the wall is in the sun for much of the day, select one of the roses that benefits from additional heat, such as 'Gloire de Dijon' or a slightly tender China rose, such as *R.* × *odorata* 'Mutabilis'.

Climbing roses combine particularly well with other climbers, such as clematis or passion flowers. You can create some enchanting colour combinations if the plants flower at the same time, or you can choose an accompanying climber that flowers before or after the rose to extend the season of interest. For instance, the rose could support an earlier-flowering *macropetala*-type clematis or a large-flowered type, such as 'The President', which would flower at the same time as the rose.

Team light colours with dark ones, combine complementaries or use shades of the same colour. The pale pink climbing rose 'New Dawn' would work equally well with the pink clematis 'Nelly Moser' or the deep purple 'Jackmanii'. Try the rich red climber 'Guinée' with the smoky pink clematis 'Purpurea Plena Elegans', or 'Golden Showers' with the rich violet clematis 'Haku-ôkan'. In a white garden, try the old climber 'Madame Alfred Carrière', which has a long flowering season and tolerates some shade, with the clematis 'Henryi'. Use white foxgloves (*Digitalis purpurea* f. *albiflora*) to provide vertical interest.

All climbing roses tend to become bare at the base in time. Mask this by underplanting with shallow-rooting perennials such as catmint (*Nepeta*), lambs' ears (*Stachys byzantina*), hostas or lady's mantle (*Alchemilla mollis*).

If you are restricted for space and have no more than a small patio garden, or even a balcony or roof garden, you can still enjoy climbing roses by choosing from one of the miniature climbers, such as 'Laura Ford' or 'Nice Day', which are easily grown in a large container such as a half-barrel (see Planting a climbing rose in a container).

■ BELOW
A triumvirate of climbers: rose, clematis and jasmine smother a wall.

Plant Directory

In the following gallery, roses are arranged alphabetically within groups as follows:

Rambling roses Usually large, rampant roses with a single, though generally spectacular, flush of flowers around mid-summer, often highly scented.

Climbing roses Usually repeat-flowering roses. They are subdivided as follows:

Large climbers Roses that reach a height of 6m (20ft) or more and are suitable for growing into trees, on large pergolas or against walls.

Medium-growing climbers Roses that do not normally exceed 5m (16½ft). They may be grown against walls and fences and on pergolas.

Shorter-growing climbers (the largest group) Roses that normally stay below 4m (13ft). Most are suitable for growing against walls and on pergolas. Many are stiffly upright and are best grown on pillars. Others, usually of recent introduction, may be grown in containers. Some roses included in this group can also be grown as shrubs if they are pruned hard.

The dimensions of height and spread given are approximate and are what the rose may be expected to achieve given good cultivation. They may vary depending on soil type, climate and season. The date the rose was first cultivated is given when known.

Rambling roses

■ ABOVE
'ALBÉRIC BARBIER'

A vigorous rambling rose, introduced in 1900. It will grow to 5m (16½ft) high and 3m (10ft) across. In early to mid-summer, it produces masses of double, rosette, creamy white, scented flowers. The leaves are glossy and often persist through the winter. 'Albéric Barbier' is a wonderful sight when in full flower, and tolerates some shade.

■ BELOW

'AMERICAN PILLAR'

A vigorous rambling rose, introduced in 1902. It will grow to 5m (16½ft) high and 2.4m (8ft) across. In mid-summer it produces clusters of reddish-pink single flowers with white centres amid glossy leaves. 'American Pillar' was a popular rose and is often found in old gardens but has fallen out of favour, perhaps because it flowers only once, lacks scent and is susceptible to mildew.

■ ABOVE

'ALBERTINE'

A vigorous rambling rose, introduced in 1921, which will grow to 5m (16½ft) high and 4m (13ft) across. The fully double, cupped, heavily scented pink flowers, borne in a single flush in mid-summer, open from copper-tinted buds; they become untidy as they age. The leaves, tinged red on emergence, are small and thick. 'Albertine' has talon-like thorns and is particularly prone to mildew in dry summers; nevertheless it remains one of the most highly rated of all ramblers due to the profusion of its flowers and their potent fragrance.

■ LEFT

'BOBBIE JAMES'

A vigorous rambling rose, introduced in 1961, which will grow to 10m (30ft) high and 6m (20ft) across. In summer it covers itself with clusters of small, white, semi-double flowers that are sweetly scented. The leaves are glossy green. 'Bobbie James' is an excellent choice for growing into a large tree. Otherwise, use only where space permits.

■ RIGHT

'RAMBLING RECTOR'

A vigorous rambling rose, introduced before 1912, which will grow to 6m (20ft) high and across. In summer it covers itself with clusters of small, single, white, fragrant flowers; small red hips follow in autumn. The leaves are glossy bright green. 'Rambling Rector', an impressive sight in maturity when in full flower, is suitable for growing into a large tree.

■ ABOVE AND INSET

'SEAGULL'

A rambling rose, introduced in 1907, which will grow to 6m (20ft) high and 4m (13ft) across. In summer it produces a single flush of clusters of small, white, single to semi-double, fragrant flowers. The leaves are greyish-green. Less vigorous than some other similar roses, 'Seagull' can be grown into a small to medium-sized tree.

■ RIGHT

'VEILCHENBLAU'

(syn. 'Blue Rambler', 'Violet Blue')
A vigorous rambling rose, introduced in 1909, which will grow to 4m (13ft) high and across. In mid-summer it produces clusters of sweetly scented, semi-double, violet-pink flowers with yellow stamens. The flowers fade to purplish-grey. The leaves are glossy and light green. More modest than most ramblers, 'Veilchenblau' is suitable for a small garden. It is best grown where there is some shelter from the midday sun.

Large climbers

■ BELOW

'CLIMBING QUEEN ELIZABETH'

Climbing rose introduced in 1957. Shapely, high-centred, fully double, lightly scented, clear-pink flowers are freely produced from summer to autumn. The leaves are leathery and glossy. Height 6m (20ft), spread 3m (19ft). 'Climbing Queen Elizabeth' is a sport of the popular shrub rose 'Queen Elizabeth'.

■ ABOVE

'CLIMBING CÉCILE BRÜNNER'

A vigorous climbing rose, introduced in 1894, which will grow to 6m (20ft) high and across. Over a long period in summer, large clusters of small, fully double, sweetly scented, pale pink flowers open from pointed buds. The leaves are plentiful. 'Climbing Cécile Brünner', a sport of the dainty China rose 'Cécile Brünner', is a good choice for growing through a tree; in other situations it can disappoint, since flowering is not always profuse.

■ LEFT
'MADAME GRÉGOIRE STAECHELIN'

A vigorous climbing rose, introduced in 1927. It will grow to 6m (20ft) high and 4m (13ft) across. In early summer fully double, rounded, sweetly scented, warm-pink flowers with slightly frilled petals are borne in profusion in hanging clusters. The leaves are matt green. 'Madame Grégoire Staechelin' flowers once only, but at its peak it can be sumptuous; it has large, showy hips that redden in autumn.

■ RIGHT
'MERMAID'

A vigorous climbing rose, introduced in 1918. It will grow to 6m (20ft) high and across. From mid-summer until autumn single, pale yellow, fragrant flowers open from pointed buds to reveal prominent golden stamens that persist after the petals have fallen. The leaves are glossy and semi-evergreen or evergreen, depending on the season; the stems are viciously thorny. 'Mermaid' tolerates some shade and is best grown where it gets shelter from hard frosts. Although the flowers are not abundant, they are beautiful.

Medium-growing climbers

■ LEFT

'CLIMBING ENA HARKNESS'

A vigorous climbing large-flowered rose, introduced in 1954. It will grow to 5m (16½ft) high and 2.4m (8ft) across. The rich scarlet, fully double, fragrant, urn-shaped flowers hang elegantly from the stems and are borne over a long period from summer to autumn. The leaves are semi-glossy. 'Climbing Ena Harkness', a sport of the bush rose 'Ena Harkness', needs a warm, sheltered site to give of its best.

■ RIGHT

'CLIMBING ICEBERG'

A climbing cluster-flowered (floribunda) rose, introduced in 1968. It will grow to 5m (16½ft) or more high and across. From summer to autumn clusters of lightly scented, creamy white, cupped, double flowers are produced among abundant, glossy light green leaves. The stems are virtually thornless. 'Climbing Iceberg', a sport of the popular shrub rose 'Iceberg', is among the most reliable of modern climbers and is a good choice for clothing a wall.

■ LEFT

'CLIMBING PEACE'

A climbing rose, introduced in 1951, and a sport of the popular large-flowered bush rose 'Peace'. It will grow to 5m (16½ft) high and 1.2m (4ft) across. The large, fully double, fragrant flowers are creamy yellow flushed with pink, and appear from summer to autumn. The abundant leaves are large and glossy.

■ RIGHT

'DESPREZ À FLEURS JAUNES'

(syn. 'Jaune Desprez') A climbing noisette rose, introduced in 1830, which will grow to 5m (16½ft) high and across. In summer it produces fully double, quartered, fragrant, warm creamy yellow flowers that open virtually flat. The leaves are light green. Best trained against a warm wall, this rose is an exquisite climber.

■ LEFT

'GLOIRE DE DIJON'

A vigorous climbing tea rose, introduced in 1853. It will grow to 5m (16½ft) high and 4m (13ft) across. The striking, fully double, fragrant, quartered-rosette, buff-apricot flowers are produced over a long period from early summer to autumn. The leaves are tinged red on emergence in spring. 'Gloire de Dijon', one of the oldest climbing roses and commonly known as the old glory rose, is still widely grown; it appreciates a sunny, sheltered site.

■ BELOW

'MADAME ALFRED CARRIÈRE'

A climbing noisette rose, introduced in 1879, which will grow to 5m (16½ft) high and 3m (10ft) across. From summer to autumn the creamy white, double, cupped, fragrant flowers are freely produced on almost thornless stems. The leaves are large and pale green. 'Madame Alfred Carrière', a dependable rose, tolerates some shade and is excellent for growing into a tree or for covering a wall.

Shorter-growing climbers

■ ABOVE

'ALOHA'

A climbing large-flowered rose, introduced in 1949. It will grow to 3m (10ft) high and 2.4m (8ft) across. The cupped, fully double, light pink, rain-resistant flowers are borne from summer to autumn. The leaves are dark green. 'Aloha' is suitable for growing in a container.

■ ABOVE RIGHT

'BREATH OF LIFE'

A climbing large-flowered rose, introduced in 1982. It will grow to 2.4m (8ft) high and 2.1m (7ft) across. From summer to autumn it bears fully double, rounded, fragrant pink flowers. This rose can be grown as a shrub with hard pruning.

■ LEFT

'BLAIRII NUMBER TWO'

A Bourbon climber introduced in 1845. It produces an abundance of large, cupped, fully double, sweetly scented flowers in mid-summer that are pale silvery-pink with deeper pink centres. The leaves are matt dark green and rough to the touch. Height 4m (13ft), spread 2m (6½ft). Unlike most other Bourbons, 'Blairii Number Two' will produce few, if any, further blooms in autumn.

■ ABOVE

'CASINO'

Climbing rose introduced in 1963. Over a long period in summer the double, fragrant, soft yellow flowers open from pointed, deep yellow buds. The leaves are glossy dark green. Height 3m (10ft), spread 2.1m (7ft). 'Casino' appreciates a warm site sheltered from cold winds. It can be grown as a shrub with hard pruning.

■ RIGHT

'CHAPLIN'S PINK CLIMBER'

A vigorous climbing rose, introduced in 1928, which will grow to 4m (13ft) high and 2.4m (8ft) across. From summer to autumn it produces semi-double, lightly scented, bright pink flowers with prominent golden stamens. The leaves are mid-green. It is sometimes sold as 'Chaplin's Pink'.

■ ABOVE LEFT

'CLIMBING BLUE MOON'

A climbing large-flowered rose, introduced in 1964. It will grow to 3m (10ft) high and 1.8m (6ft) across. Throughout summer it produces fully double, scented, lilac-mauve flowers that appear bluer when it is grown in full sun. The leaves are glossy green. 'Climbing Blue Moon' is a sport of the large-flowered bush rose 'Blue Moon'.

■ ABOVE RIGHT

'COMPASSION'

A climbing large-flowered rose, introduced in 1973, which will grow to 3m (10ft) high and 2.4m (8ft) across. From summer to autumn it produces shapely, rounded, fully double, sweetly scented, warm apricot-pink flowers. The leaves are dark green. 'Compassion' is excellent grown on a pillar.

■ RIGHT

'COMPLICATA'

Vigorous gallica rose, of unknown origin, suitable for training as a climber. In mid-summer it carries masses of saucer-shaped, sweetly scented, single, translucent pink flowers with white centres and golden stamens. The leaves are greyish green. Height and spread to 2.4m (8ft) or more. 'Complicata' is best suited to an informal planting, allowed to grow into trees and shrubs.

■ ABOVE LEFT

'CONSTANCE SPRY'

A shrub rose, introduced in 1961, suitable for training as a climber. It will grow to 3m (10ft) high and across. In mid-summer it produces a profusion of large, cupped, fully double, richly scented, warm-pink flowers. The leaves are coarse and greyish-green. Despite its single flush of flowers, 'Constance Spry' is one of the most desirable of modern climbers and is spectacular at its peak; it tolerates some shade.

■ ABOVE RIGHT

'CRIMSON DESCANT'

A climbing rose, introduced in 1972, which will grow to 3m (10ft) high and 1.2m (4ft) across. From summer to autumn it produces masses of double, lightly scented, bright crimson flowers. The foliage is glossy green. 'Crimson Descant' is a reliably healthy rose, tolerates some shade, and is suitable for a pillar.

■ ABOVE

'DUBLIN BAY'

A climbing rose, introduced in 1976, which has a height and spread of 2.1m (7ft). From summer to autumn clusters of double, lightly scented, almost fluorescent red flowers are produced amid healthy, glossy, large leaves. 'Dublin Bay' is a good choice where space is limited, since the growth tends to be upright.

■ ABOVE

'DANSE DU FEU'

A vigorous climbing rose, introduced in 1954, which will grow to 2.4m (8ft) high and across. From summer to autumn it bears clusters of double, rounded, lightly scented, luminous red flowers among glossy, bronze-tinged, dark green leaves. 'Danse du Feu', a popular and free-flowering rose, is prone to blackspot.

■ RIGHT

'GOLDEN SHOWERS'

A climbing rose, introduced in 1957, which will grow to 3m (10ft) high and 1.8m (6ft) across. From summer to autumn it produces clusters of double (but with few petals), lightly scented, yellow flowers. The leaves are glossy dark green. 'Golden Showers' performs well in a variety of situations and tolerates some shade.

■ LEFT

'HANDEL'

A vigorous climbing rose, introduced in 1965. It will grow to 3m (10ft) high and 2.1m (7ft) across. Double, urn-shaped, lightly scented flowers with cream petals edged with pink, are produced from mid-summer to autumn. The dark green leaves are tinged bronze. 'Handel' is valued for the unique colouring of its flowers; with hard pruning it can be grown as a shrub. Blackspot may be a problem.

■ ABOVE RIGHT

'HIGHFIELD'

A climbing rose, introduced in 1981, and a sport of 'Compassion'. It will grow to 3m (10ft) high and 2.4m (8ft) across. From summer to autumn it produces shapely, rounded, fully double, fragrant, primrose-yellow flowers. The leaves are dark green.

■ LEFT

'LAURA FORD'

A miniature climbing rose, introduced in 1990. It will grow to 2.1m (7ft) high and 1.2m (4ft) across. From summer to autumn it produces clusters of small, lightly scented, yellow flowers among small, shiny, dark green leaves. An excellent choice for a small garden, 'Laura Ford' is also suitable for growing in a container.

■ ABOVE

'LOUISE ODIER'

A Bourbon rose, introduced in 1851, suitable for training as a climber and best with some support. It will grow to 2.4m (8ft) high and 1.8m (6ft) across. From mid-summer to autumn it produces clusters of cupped, fully double, strongly scented, lilac-tinted, warm pink flowers. The leaves are greyish-green.

■ ABOVE

'MAIGOLD'

A vigorous climbing pimpinellifolia hybrid, introduced in 1953, which will grow to 2.4m (8ft) high and across. In early summer, semi-double, cupped, sweetly scented, rich-yellow flowers are produced in clusters, usually in a single flush. The leaves are leathery and glossy. 'Maigold', a tough and hardy rose, is valued for its early flowering and resistance to disease.

■ BELOW

'MORNING JEWEL'

A vigorous climbing rose, introduced in 1968, which will grow to 3m (10ft) high and 2.4m (8ft) across. Clusters of glowing-pink, double, cupped, lightly scented flowers are freely produced in mid-summer; the autumn display is less profuse. The leaves are glossy dark green. Generally a healthy rose, 'Morning Jewel' can be grown as a shrub with hard pruning.

■ LEFT

'MADAME ISAAC PEREIRE'

Bourbon rose introduced in 1881 suitable for training as a climber. From summer to autumn huge, richly fragrant, luminous cerise-pink flowers open as quartered rosettes but become muddled as they mature, especially those of the first flush. The leaves are matt, dark green. Height 2.4m (8ft), spread 2m (6½ft). 'Madame Isaac Pereire' is one of the most strongly scented of all roses. It can be prone to mildew.

■ ABOVE

'OLD BLUSH CHINA'

China rose, introduced from China around 1752 but undoubtedly much older, suitable for training as a climber. From summer to early winter, it produces double, cupped, fragrant, clear pink flowers amid elegant, pointed leaves. Height 2.4m (8ft), spread 1.5m (5ft). 'Old Blush China' rewards careful cultivation by flowering until the first frosts.

■ ABOVE

'PARKDIREKTOR RIGGERS'

A vigorous climbing rose, introduced in 1957, which will grow to 4m (13ft) high and across. From summer to autumn it produces semi-double, lightly scented, glowing crimson flowers that have prominent yellow stamens. The leaves are glossy dark green. 'Parkdirektor Riggers' is valued for its disease-resistance and long flowering season.

■ RIGHT

X *ODORATA* 'MUTABILIS'

A China rose of uncertain parentage, introduced from China some time before 1894, although it may be much older. It is suitable for training as a climber and will grow to 3m (10ft) high and 1.8m (6ft) across. The single, cupped, lightly scented flowers are borne over a long period from summer to autumn. They are of unique colouring: flame-orange in bud, they open to coppery yellow, then fade to pink, the pink deepening to purple as they age. The leaves are dark green and glossy. *R.* × *odorata* (sometimes sold as *R. chinensis* 'Mutabilis' or simply 'Mutabilis' appreciates a warm site, and in cold climates is best in full sun against a wall.

■ LEFT

'PINK PERPÉTUÉ'

A vigorous climbing rose, introduced in 1965, which will grow to 3m (10ft) high and 2.4m (8ft) across. The lightly scented flowers, which are borne from summer to autumn, are double, cupped to rosette, and have petals that are light pink with darker bases. The leaves are leathery and dark green. 'Pink Perpétué' has a spreading habit that makes it suitable for covering a wall; it can also be grown as a shrub if it is pruned hard. Rust may be a problem.

■ RIGHT

'SOMBREUIL' (CLIMBING FORM)

Climbing rose introduced in 1850. From summer to autumn it produces flat, quartered rosette, sweetly scented flowers that are creamy white tinged with flesh pink as they age. The leaves are mid-green. Height 2.4m (8ft), spread 1.5m (5ft). The flowers of 'Sombreuil' can be spoilt by wet weather; nevertheless, it is a rose of considerable distinction.

■ BELOW

'SCHOOLGIRL'

A climbing rose which will grow to 3m (10ft) high and 2.4m (8ft) across. From summer to autumn the fully double, fragrant flowers open from urn-shaped buds. The large leaves are not plentiful. Although not free-flowering, 'Schoolgirl' is valued for its scent and unusual orange flower colour.

■ ABOVE LEFT

'SOUVENIR DE LA MALMAISON' (CLIMBING FORM)

Climbing rose introduced in 1893. The fully double, quartered rosette, fragrant flowers are pale pink, ageing to white, and are produced from summer to autumn. The leaves are small and dark green. Height 4m (13ft), spread 2.4m (8ft). 'Souvenir de la Malmaison' is named in honour of Empress Josephine's famous garden at Malmaison. The silk-textured flowers may be spoilt by wet weather.

■ ABOVE RIGHT

'SYMPATHIE'

A climbing large-flowered rose, introduced in 1964. It will grow to 3m (10ft) or more high and 2.4m (8ft) across. Double, fragrant, bright red flowers are produced in profusion from early summer to early autumn. 'Sympathie' tolerates some shade and is disease-resistant.

■ LEFT

'TYNWALD'

A large-flowered rose, introduced in 1979, suitable for training as a climber. It will grow to 2.4m (8ft) high and 1.2m (4ft) across. The very fragrant, creamy white flowers are shaded ivory at the centre and appear from summer to autumn. The luxuriant foliage is dark green. 'Tynwald' is a disease-resistant rose and is good for cut flowers.

■ RIGHT

'WHITE COCKADE'

A climbing rose, introduced in 1969, which will grow to 2.1m (7ft) high and 1.5m (5ft) across. Fully double, rounded, slightly scented, white flowers are produced almost continuously from summer to autumn. The dark green leaves are large and glossy. 'White Cockade' is particularly valued for its perfectly shaped flowers. It may be grown as a shrub, if pruned well, and it is a good choice for a container or growing up a short pillar.

■ LEFT

'WILLIAM LOBB'

Moss rose introduced in 1855, suitable for training as a climber. In mid-summer the large, double, rosette, heavily scented, magenta-purple flowers open from heavily mossed buds, then fade to violet-grey. The dark green leaves are produced in abundance. Height and spread 2m (6½ft). The range of tones in the flowers of 'William Lobb' as they mature and fade is remarkable.

■ ABOVE

'ZÉPHIRINE DROUHIN'

A Bourbon rose, introduced either in 1868 or 1873, which will grow to about 3m (10ft) high and 1.8m (6ft) across. During summer and autumn it produces clusters of double, cupped to flat, deep purplish-pink flowers which are strongly fragranced. The leaves are glossy light green and the stems are thornless. 'Zéphirine Drouhin', sometimes called the "thornless rose", can be grown as a shrub if it is pruned hard.

MINIATURE ROSES

At one time a rose garden was the prerogative of gardeners with masses of space to devote to the culture of one of the world's favourite flowers. The advent of miniature and patio roses, however, has brought a complete sea change in rose growing. Their versatility and compact size, combined with their ability to produce an abundance of beautiful blooms over very long periods – often almost continuously from summer to the first frosts of autumn – has brought the joys of rose growing to gardeners with even the tiniest of plots. There can be no doubt that many more of these delightful plants will be produced in the future.

■ PREVIOUS PAGE
The small, double blooms of 'Little Flirt' are bright pink, with a paler pink petal reverse.

■ RIGHT
Diminutive roses, such as the delicate 'White Pet', bring grace and beauty to even the smallest of gardens.

The history of miniature roses

Until the end of the 17th century, nearly all of the roses grown in European gardens flowered once only, around mid-summer. These are some of the most ancient roses: the Albas, Gallicas, Damasks and Centifolias, along with their mossy sports, the Moss roses. Many are still grown and are much loved to this day for their pure colours and heavenly fragrance. But the introduction of *Rosa chinensis*, the China rose, revolutionized rose breeding in Europe, for it is this species and its variants that possessed the invaluable characteristic of 'remontancy', or repeat-flowering.

In 1781, a pink-flowered China rose known as 'Old Blush China' (now known as *R.* × *odorata* 'Pallida') was introduced to the Netherlands from India. Several years later, the British East India Company brought the crimson-flowered *R. semperflorens* or 'Slater's Crimson China' to Britain. The importance of these plants in rose breeding can hardly be overestimated. The genetic legacy of these two Chinese roses is expressed in almost all of the roses that flower repeatedly today.

In the early years, the Chinese roses were crossed with European roses to yield the repeat-flowering Bourbons, Portlands, Noisettes and Tea roses and, finally, the Hybrid Perpetuals, the elegant forerunners of the modern Hybrid Teas (now called large-flowered bush roses). The era of the modern rose began in 1867 with the introduction of the first Hybrid Tea, 'La France', which was probably as a result of a chance cross between a Hybrid Perpetual and a Tea rose.

Further developments followed rapidly. By introducing the genes of *R. moschata* and *R. multiflora* to those of *R. chinensis,* a new, very hardy race – the dwarf Polyanthas – eventually emerged around 1900.

■ ABOVE
Rosa 'Old Blush China' was one of the most important introductions, bringing repeat-flowering genes to modern roses.

■ OPPOSITE LEFT
***Rosa* 'Rouletii', syn. *R. chinensis* var. *minima*, also known as the Pygmy rose.**

■ RIGHT
***Rosa* 'White Flower Carpet' produces clusters of small, double, lightly scented, white flowers from summer to autumn.**

These were first developed by the Poulsen nurseries in Denmark. The eventual result was the Floribundas, or cluster-flowered bush roses.

It is worth bearing in mind the origin of these roses. To be so successful in the harsh winter climates of continental and northern Europe, these compact and floriferous bushes needed to be extremely tough and hardy. Again, this constitutional legacy is one that benefits growers of modern roses; their descendants, the dwarf cluster-flowered bushes, better known as 'Patio roses', are very cold-tolerant. Most derive from crossings of Floribundas with dwarf Polyanthas and miniature roses. Their group name is somewhat unfortunate, for although they are undoubtedly of suitable proportions for growing in pots to decorate a patio, it scarcely describes their versatility in gardens.

Origins of miniature roses

The origins of the true miniature roses are still mysterious, although many experts agree that the original miniatures were probably diminutive sports (mutations) of a China rose; indeed, *R. chinensis* seems, throughout its long history, to have proved a particularly valuable species. After its introduction to Europe, the earliest miniatures appear to have been grown primarily as houseplants. What is certain is that the discovery, by a Swiss army officer named Roulet in 1918, of tiny roses of this type decorating the window ledges of Swiss chalets stimulated the interest of Dutch and Spanish hybridizers. The genes of *Rosa* 'Rouletii' (syn. *R. chinensis* var. *minima,* now known as 'Pompon de Paris') are obviously present in many of the modern miniatures grown in gardens today.

The 1980s saw the advent of a new rose revolution: the creation of the so-called ground-cover roses that would reduce the need for weeding by shading out some weeds with their dense-leaved habit. Again, the term 'ground-cover' does little justice to their versatility.

The development of the ground-cover roses and miniature roses has continued apace in the UK, in continental Europe and, especially for the miniatures, in the United States. Given this provenance, you can be sure that these roses will be cold-hardy in all but the most severe of climates. The increase in popularity of these small roses went hand-in-hand with the general reduction in the size of gardens in the latter part of the 20th century. Having found a considerable market demand, there is no doubt that their ranks will swell in future years. As yet, there are relatively few miniature climbers, but breeders are working hard on the case.

Using small roses in the garden

For many years we became used to seeing beds and borders filled exclusively with roses in serried, formal ranks, emerging stiffly upright above sterile areas of bare soil. Indeed, many rose growers still regard this as the 'correct' way to grow them. While the formal rose bed still undoubtedly has its place, it is increasingly difficult not to view this treatment of roses as singularly lacking in imagination, given the diversity of size, habit and flowering period of roses as a group. The new roses, especially the smaller-growing ones, prove exceptionally versatile, and their uses in gardens are limited only by the imagination of the grower and the chosen style of garden.

■ ABOVE
Tightly packed clusters of flowers are typical of the Patio roses.

■ BELOW LEFT
A low ribbon of roses flanking a path draws the eye to an elegant focal point.

Miniature roses

Ranging in height from the tiniest, such as Rosa 'Rouletii' at 12cm (5in) tall, to the general run of miniatures at around 25–40cm (10–16in) in height, perhaps the primary consideration when using miniatures is that they should be placed where they can be appreciated at close quarters. While the larger cultivars can be put to much the same uses as the Patio roses, the smallest ones are at their best in containers that bring

■ RIGHT
Ground-cover roses cascade over the edge of a raised bed. Raised beds allow miniature roses to be brought closer to eye level.

them up to, or very nearly up to, eye level. They are perfect in pots, troughs and window boxes, and they are even tough enough to be grown on high balconies in this way. Miniatures are also very useful for hanging baskets, either on their own or in mixed plantings with trailing annuals, such as lobelia, or the long, cascading stems of *Helichrysum petiolare* (syn. *H. petiolatum*), with its soft, sage-grey leaves. They are equally at home in small raised beds, which is a particularly valuable way of growing them in small courtyard gardens, where open areas of soil are absent or at a premium. Some growers use miniatures in the rock garden. While their scale suits this type of site, they can be difficult to place there, since their highly bred style seldom associates well with alpine plants, which have a more natural habit of growth.

Many older cultivars were originally used as pot plants for decorating the home. Indeed, their revival in popularity has seen increased sales of miniatures as houseplants in supermarkets and garden centres, although the choice here is often fairly limited and they are seldom sold as named varieties. While their colour and diminutive beauty can clearly be appreciated at close quarters when grown as houseplants, if they are to achieve any degree of permanence, they must have excellent light. Most perform best if given periodic spells in a well-lit conservatory, or if moved to a sunny spot outdoors during the summer months.

Patio roses

Dwarf cluster-flowered roses, popularly known as Patio roses, are neat, compact little bushes, which are usually covered in wide clusters of flowers throughout the summer, until stopped by the first hard frosts of autumn. With most in the size range of 40–75cm (16–30in) tall by as much across, these small, free-flowering bushes earn their keep in even the tiniest sites. The term 'Patio rose' suggests unjustified restrictions on their use. They are, indeed, ideal for planting in terracotta pots, tubs and urns, and they will provide many months of pleasure when they are placed on patios, balconies and terraces and in porches, but they have a range of other uses, too.

Patio roses are often used as massed bedding in a formal bed or border, and this is an ideal way of growing them if solid blocks of long-lasting colour are needed. Most have the advantages of hardiness and a healthy constitution, which is important in massed plantings, where uniformity of colour and performance is an absolute requirement. This uniformity can

■ LEFT

Trailing ground-cover roses, grown as weeping standards, can be trained both to decorate a hedge and frame an entrance.

■ ABOVE

Roses do not need to be trailing to be effective in hanging baskets, as these ground-cover roses demonstrate.

also be put to good use when they are planted as low hedging or as edging to a border or pathway.

When grown as a single or double row flanking a path, they provide a low, continuous ribbon of colour that is beautiful in its own right. They also perform an invaluable design function by drawing the eye along the planting scheme, which may then terminate in an attractive focal point, such as a rose arch, statue or tall, elegant container, where climbing roses can continue the theme.

Ground-cover roses

These are among the most versatile of the smaller roses, especially the repeat-flowering cultivars of more modern breeding. Ground-cover roses come in two main types, both equally hardy: the compact, very bushy and slightly spreading types, such as 'Laura Ashley' (syn. 'Chewharia'); and the trailing ground-cover roses, such as 'Nozomi' (syn. 'Heideröslein'), which have long, flexible stems that root where they touch the ground. The spreading growth tends to form a low mound of foliage that is perfect for the front of a shrub or mixed border, mixing well with shrubs and perennials.

Ground-cover roses, especially the trailing sorts, are perfect for clothing sunny banks, especially those that are awkward and inaccessible, since most require little maintenance or pruning. Their trailing habit is displayed to great advantage if allowed to cascade from a height: each flexible stem will be wreathed along its entire length with bloom for much of the summer.

They can be grown over retaining walls or from the top of a terrace, planted in tall pots and urns, or in large, moss-lined hanging baskets. Many are also available as standards, grafted on to the top of a long, straight stem to give a graceful, weeping effect. Moreover, if you use them in any of these ways where they can be reflected in still water, you double their beauty instantly.

Their effectiveness as ground cover relies on the density of their foliage to exclude light and so reduce weed growth beneath them. Since many are deciduous, some experts consider 'ground-cover' a misleading term, for the growth of some weed species continues unabated during the cold months, when the roses are leafless. If they are to be effective as ground cover, thorough preparation in advance is absolutely fundamental to their success.

They must be planted in very clean, weed-free soil and top-dressed with a weed suppressant mulch, such as chipped bark, or planted through a sheet mulch of landscaping fabric.

Dwarf Polyanthas, Chinas and Centifolias

The small bushes in this group often have a graceful habit, with airy sprays of bloom that associate particularly well with herbaceous perennials and with other shrubs in a mixed border. They are ideal for cottage-garden style plantings, and their restricted height makes them particularly suitable for low hedging, useful when you need to create barriers between different parts of the garden. They also make ideal container plants, with an elegant habit that suits a range of pots, tubs and urns. Use them to decorate a patio or courtyard, to create a focal point or to mark a change in style or level within the garden. Alternatively, pairs can be used to flank an entrance.

Most of this group of small roses, which includes the Polyantha 'Cécile Brünner' (syn. 'Mignon', 'Sweetheart Rose') and its sport 'Perle d'Or' (syn. 'Yellow Cécile Brünner'), have been grown in gardens for over a century, and are hardy and reliable.

■ RIGHT
In this cottage garden, roses blend perfectly with love-in-a-mist (*Nigella damascena*).

Miniature climbers

In small gardens, where space is inevitably restricted, these climbers, which seldom grow to more than 2.1m (7ft) tall and 1.2m (4ft) across, are perfect for clothing walls or fences, either to form a feature in their own right or to be a backdrop for other foreground plantings. Grown against a wall or on free-standing architectural structures, such as pyramids or tripods, they provide a strong vertical element in a design.

Most miniature climbers flower almost continuously throughout summer and have the advantage of remaining well clothed with foliage almost down to ground level. This is seldom true of large climbers, which tend to become bare at the base unless they are trained firmly to the horizontal during their early years.

In courtyards, where soil beds are impracticable for reasons of space, miniature climbers can be grown in large pots or tubs. As with all types of container cultivation, however, easy access to a water source is essential. Plants in pots dry out rapidly in hot weather, especially if warm, dry conditions are prolonged, and you need to check them daily.

■ ABOVE
The elegant rose garden at Chatsworth, in Derbyshire, England, complete with formal clipped hedges and pillars clothed in magnificent climbing roses.

■ LEFT
A miniature climber looks charming twining up a rustic wooden support.

Miniature roses in the home

Miniature and small roses are perfect for cutting and using in posies and other diminutive arrangements. They last best if cut early in the day, because then the stems are turgid (full of water). Leave as long a length of stem as possible, remove the lowest leaves and thorns, and plunge them up to their necks in cold water for a few hours before arranging. Immediately before arranging, trim the stem with a slanting cut while still under water. You may need to provide the support of florists' foam, wire mesh or a scrunch of wire netting for arrangements.

Roses of most colours blend well with shades of blue, as provided by the spires of delphiniums, or for a cottage-garden style, by scabious, nigella, cornflowers, or larkspur. Gypsophila, with its airy panicles of small white flowers, adds an element of textural contrast. Flowers in the apricot-pink to salmon band of the spectrum look particularly good against bronze or purple foliage, such as that of copper beech, *Fagus sylvatica f. purpurea*, or *Cotinus coggygria*. Those in the clear pink and crimson-red range are set off perfectly against the silver-grey leaves of plants like the artemisias and lavenders.

When growing miniatures as pot plants, use a loam-based mix (such as John Innes No. 2 or a commercially prepared planting mix), and provide bright light but avoid exposure to hot midday sun through glass, which may scorch the plant. Keep evenly moist and feed with a balanced fertilizer at two- to three-week intervals throughout the growing season. Indoor roses suffer from lack of light, and may eventually cease to grow and flower well, but during the summer months they can be moved outdoors or transferred to a site with high light levels, such as a conservatory. Prune and deadhead as for outdoor roses.

■ TOP LEFT AND RIGHT **Very versatile, miniature roses are at home in dried arrangements in containers.**

■ RIGHT **Plunge freshly cut roses up to their necks in cool fresh water for a few hours.**

■ LEFT

'ANGELA RIPPON'
(SYN. 'OCARINA', 'OCARU')

This miniature bush rose has a dense-leaved, upright and bushy habit and is well clothed in glossy dark green, healthy foliage. Throughout summer, it bears clusters of small, rounded, fully double flowers of deep, rich salmon-pink that have a light fragrance. The healthy foliage is a glossy dark green. Good for pots, large window boxes and low edging or hedging. Height 45cm (18in), spread 30cm (12in).

The selection of roses described here are hardy and reliable, and as well as being beautiful, most produce vivacious blooms over many summer months. Most are readily available from garden centres, although a few will require a little searching out from specialist nurseries. Their dimensions are given as guidelines only; sizes always vary slightly according to variable growing conditions.

■ RIGHT

'ANNA FORD'
(SYN. 'HARPICCOLO')

An award-winning Patio rose of compact habit and with a notably good health record. The glossy, dark green leaves provide an admirable foil for the clusters of vibrant orange-red, semi-double, urn-shaped flowers that are produced from summer to autumn. Good for containers, borders and low hedging. Height 45cm (18in), spread 40cm (16in).

■ RIGHT

'APRICOT SUMMER' (SYN. 'KORPAPIRO')

A Patio rose of neat, compact habit that flowers freely throughout the summer months, bearing a profusion of small, double, rounded, salmon-apricot blooms in many-flowered clusters. Useful for pots, window boxes, beds and border edging. Height 40cm (16in), spread 40cm (16in).

■ ABOVE

'AVON' (SYN. 'POULMULTI')

A low, creeping ground-cover rose of compact habit with mid-green leaves. The creeping stems are wreathed with clusters of flat, semi-double, lightly scented blush-pink then pearly-white flowers from summer to autumn. It is also available as a weeping standard. Ideal for clothing awkward banks or for a flowering cascade over a wall. Height 30cm (12in), spread 90cm (36in).

■ BELOW

'BABY LOVE' (SYN. 'SCRIVLUV')

A bushy, upright Patio rose with dense, mid-green foliage and clusters of cupped, single, short-stemmed, bright yellow flowers throughout summer. An exceptionally healthy and floriferous little rose, which, although really rather tall for most containers, is perfect for beds, borders and low hedging. Height 1m (39in), spread 75cm (30in).

■ BELOW

'CAPTAIN SCARLET'

A stiffly upright miniature climber of compact habit with good disease-resistance; unlike most other larger climbers, it remains clothed to the base with flowers and foliage. The semi-double, rounded, bright red, rather muddled flowers are produced repeatedly from summer to autumn, set off beautifully by dark green foliage that becomes flushed with copper tints in cold weather. Height 2.2m (7ft), spread 1.2m (4ft).

■ ABOVE

'BALLERINA'

A compact Polyantha shrub rose, one of the older small roses, bred in 1937. It has a compact, leafy, upright habit and bears wide clusters of cupped, single, pale pink, white-eyed blooms throughout summer into autumn. A notably floriferous award-winner, but with little scent, it is ideal for borders and low hedging and makes a good specimen for small gardens. Height up to 1.5m (5ft), spread 1m (39in).

■ RIGHT

'BROADLANDS' (SYN. 'TANMIRSCH')

A vigorous, spreading ground-cover rose forming low mounds of glossy, dark green foliage are wreathed in double, rounded, soft sulphur-yellow, sweetly scented flowers throughout summer into autumn. The colour yellow is unusual among ground-cover roses. It is ideal for clothing awkward banks or for the front of a border. Height 90cm (36in), spread 1.1m (3½ft).

■ ABOVE
'CITY LIGHTS'
(SYN. 'POULGAN')

A vigorous Patio rose with dark green foliage and wide clusters of perfectly formed, urn-shaped, fully double, rich yellow blooms that are shaded with apricot at their centres. Flowering throughout summer, it is perfect for urns, troughs and pots. Its neat habit also suits border edging and low hedging. Height 60cm (24in), spread 60cm (24in).

■ RIGHT
'CIDER CUP'
(SYN. 'DICLADIDA')

A Patio rose of compact, bushy habit with dense, glossy leaves, producing many-flowered clusters of small, double, high-pointed blooms of a lovely warm apricot-pink throughout summer and autumn. The neat, upright habit is well suited to pots, as a standard and for low hedging. Height 45cm (18in), spread 30cm (12in).

■ RIGHT

'CONSERVATION' (SYN. 'COCDIMPLE')

A notably healthy Patio rose of dense, bushy habit, with small, glossy leaves and a profusion of cupped, semi-double flowers of warm apricot-pink borne in well-filled clusters from summer to autumn. A neat but vigorous grower, it is perfectly suited to containers (the colour complements natural stone and terracotta particularly well) and as low edging. Height 45cm (18in), spread 45cm (18in).

■ LEFT

'CLIMBING ORANGE SUNBLAZE' (SYN. 'CLIMBING ORANGE MEILLANDINA', 'MEIJIKATARSAR')

An aptly named miniature climber, with fully double, brilliant, blazing orange-red, rounded flowers that are produced from summer to autumn and set off to perfection against bright green foliage. It has a well-branched, upright habit and is perfect for wall training where space is limited. A climbing sport of 'Orange Sunblaze'. Height 1.5m (5ft), spread 70cm (28in).

■ RIGHT

'CRIMSON GEM'

This vigorous miniature bush is clothed throughout summer in perfectly formed, rounded, double, deep rich red flowers set off against dark, glossy foliage. It is a perfect container rose, especially good in large window boxes and containers, and is equally at home edging a bed or border. Height 45cm (18in), spread 45cm (18in).

■ ABOVE

'FESTIVAL' (SYN. 'KORDIALO')

This Patio rose has a neat, rounded habit and luxuriant, glossy dark green foliage. The sumptuously coloured crimson-scarlet double, rounded blooms open to reveal a centre of gold and silver, and the pale silvery petal reverse adds greatly to its charm. Perfect for pots, especially in pairs set to flank a doorway. Height 60cm (24in), spread 50cm (20in).

■ LEFT

'DARLING FLAME' (SYN. 'MEILUCCA', 'MINUETTO')

A colourful miniature bush producing clusters of small, rounded, double blooms of vibrant orange-red with golden anthers. It has upright growth and glossy foliage and, although free-flowering, is slightly susceptible to blackspot. Creates a brilliant ribbon of colour when used as edging, and is ideal for containers. Height 40cm (16in), spread 30cm (12in).

■ ABOVE

'FRESH PINK'

This petite Polyantha rose produces large trusses of rounded, double, clear pink flowers very freely from summer to autumn. The graceful habit is displayed to good effect in large urns or other containers, and it is equally at home lending grace and pure colour to a mixed or shrub border. Height 60–90cm (24–36in), spread 60–90cm (24–36in).

■ RIGHT

'GLORIA MUNDI'

A compact Polyantha rose with large clusters of cupped, brilliant orange-red, semi-double flowers produced almost continuously throughout the summer months. It can be used as low hedging or bedding and in containers and, unlike many roses, it will tolerate a little shade and poor soils, although flowering will be less profuse in these conditions. Height 70cm (28in), spread 70cm (28in).

■ LEFT

'HAKUUN'

A low-growing Patio rose of neat, rounded habit with exceptionally lovely, creamy white, double, rounded flowers, buff-tinted in bud and at the petal base, borne in well-filled clusters from summer to autumn. It has a pleasing light fragrance. This healthy rose would be perfect in containers sited where the flowers can be appreciated at close quarters. It is also good for cut flowers. Height 40cm (16in), spread 45cm (18in).

■ RIGHT

'HAMPSHIRE' (SYN. 'KORHAMP')

One of the 'County' series (named after English counties) of ground-cover roses, this is a dense and compact bush clothed from summer to autumn with clusters of stunning, single, slightly cupped, scarlet blooms with a white eye and a central boss of golden stamens. The flowers are followed by scarlet hips in autumn. Equally at home in containers or in open ground in beds and borders. Height 30cm (12in), spread 60cm (24in).

■ LEFT

'INDIAN SUNBLAZE' (SYN. 'CAROL-JEAN')

This is a compact miniature bush with rounded, fully double, deep pink flowers produced repeatedly from summer to autumn above fresh green foliage. Excellent for containers of all sorts and as low edging to paths and borders. Height 45cm (18in), spread 45cm (18in).

■ RIGHT

'LAURA FORD' (SYN. 'CHEWARVEL')

For the walls of a small courtyard or patio, this miniature climber's stiffly upright growth is ideal. The small, scented, semi-double, urn-shaped flowers, borne continuously from summer to autumn, are yellow, developing a hint of pink as they age, opening almost flat to reveal a boss of golden stamens. Height 2.2m (7ft), spread 1.2m (4ft).

■ BELOW

'KENT' (SYN. 'WHITE COVER', 'POULCOV', 'PYRENEES')

A compact and spreading ground-cover rose with an excellent health record and good weather resistance. Smothered in large trusses of cupped, short-stemmed, semi-double, pure white flowers from summer to autumn, it is perfect for sunny banks or for the front of mixed and shrub borders. It is also stunning if grown to cascade from tall containers or retaining walls. Height 45cm (18in), spread 1m (3ft).

■ RIGHT

'LITTLE WHITE PET' (SYN. 'WHITE PET')

A vigorous but diminutive Polyantha rose of light, airy habit, with clusters of beautifully formed, rosette-shaped flowers borne throughout summer. Pink in bud, they are white when fully open and have a light scent; the flower form is almost identical to 'Félicité Perpétue', the well-known rambler of which it is a sport. Ideal for the front of a border and very elegant in containers, it is also exquisite for miniature flower arrangements. Height 45cm (18in), spread 55cm (22in).

■ ABOVE

'LADY PENELOPE'

A stiffly upright miniature climber of neat habit, with mid-green leaves and rounded, fully double, salmon-pink flowers borne repeatedly from summer to autumn. A healthy rose that remains clothed to the base with flowers and foliage, it is ideal for walls in confined spaces and for smaller gardens. Height 2.2m (7ft), spread 1.2m (4ft).

■ LEFT

'MINI METRO' (SYN. 'FINSTAR', 'RUFIN')

A miniature bush with fresh green foliage and clusters of well-formed, rounded, fully double, apricot-orange flowers that open to reveal golden stamens. Flowering throughout summer, it is ideal for pots, window boxes and other containers. Height 40cm (16in), spread 25cm (10in).

■ ABOVE

'MR BLUEBIRD'

A miniature rose of bushy, compact habit bearing airy sprays of many small, cupped, semi-double, white-eyed flowers in shades of reddish purple, from summer to autumn. With such a novel and unusual colour, this healthy little rose is perfect for window boxes, pots and other containers, or as an edging to beds and borders. Height 30cm (12in), spread 25cm (10in).

■ RIGHT

'NICE DAY' (SYN. 'CHEWSEA', 'PATIO QUEEN')

Clusters of small, double, urn-shaped flowers of warm peachy pink with a light sweet scent are borne from summer to autumn on this petite climber. It is excellent for a low wall or trellis where space is confined; the perfectly formed buds are ideal as buttonholes and for flower arrangements. Height 2.2m (7ft), spread 1m (3ft).

■ LEFT

'NORTHAMPTONSHIRE' (SYN. 'MATTDOR')

A vigorous, low-growing ground-cover rose with dense, glossy dark green foliage and dainty sprays of perfectly formed, cupped, soft pink flowers from summer to autumn. This spreading rose has an excellent health record and is good for clothing sunny banks, for trailing over retaining walls, or for the front of a mixed border; the petite flowers make ideal boutonnières. Height 45cm (18in), spread 1m (3ft).

■ RIGHT

'ORANGES AND LEMONS' (SYN. 'MACORANLEM')

A compact cluster-flowered bush with shiny dark green leaves that are flushed copper when young. It bears heavy clusters of rounded, double flowers from summer to autumn, striped and partly coloured scarlet-orange on a creamy golden yellow ground. Perhaps too large for all but the most substantial of containers, this sunny little rose is ideal for low hedging, and massed plantings in beds and borders. Height 80cm (32in), spread 60cm (24in).

■ LEFT

'ORANGE SUNBLAZE' (SYN. 'MEIJIKATAR', 'ORANGE MEILLANDINA')

A bushy miniature rose with ample bright green foliage and profuse clusters of small, cupped, semi-double flowers of brilliant, vivid orange-red with golden centres, produced from summer to autumn. Excellent for containers of all sorts, and as low edging to paths and borders. Height 30cm (12in), spread 30cm (12in).

■ BELOW

'OXFORDSHIRE' (SYN. 'KORFULLWIND')

An award-winning, spreading ground-cover rose with cascading stems wreathed in double clear pink rounded flowers almost continuously from summer to autumn. Ideal for sunny banks, it also looks stunning when grown as a standard or in hanging baskets. Height 60cm (2ft), spread 1.5m (5ft).

■ RIGHT

'PERLE D'OR' (SYN. 'YELLOW CÉCILE BRÜNNER')

One of the older small roses, this petite Polyantha bush has a dense habit of growth, ample dark green foliage, and dainty sprays of scented, diminutive but exquisitely formed, urn-shaped flowers of creamy honey-yellow flushed with pink, lasting from summer to autumn. Almost thornless, it is ideal for a mixed border or for large urns and containers. Height 1.2m (4ft), spread 1m (3ft).

■ ABOVE

'PEEK A BOO' (SYN. 'BRASS RING', 'DICGROW')

A neat, cushion-forming Patio rose with a slightly spreading habit and well-filled clusters of small but beautifully formed, rounded, double flowers of a gentle, rich peachy apricot that gradually fade to pink as they mature. It is perfect for containers and urns, and for cutting to use in flower arrangements. Height 45cm (18in), spread 45cm (18in).

■ BELOW

'PRETTY POLLY' (SYN. 'MEITONJE', 'SWEET SUNBLAZE', 'PINK SYMPHONY')

A dense, rounded and well-named Patio rose with plentiful glossy dark green foliage. Blooming from summer to autumn, the beautifully formed, rounded, fully double flowers, borne in well-filled clusters, have a light sweet scent and are of a particularly pretty clear pink. It looks well in terracotta containers and window boxes, and would make a beautiful ribbon of colour if grown as low edging. Height 40cm (16in), spread 45cm (18in).

■ LEFT

'QUEEN MOTHER' (SYN. 'KORQUEMU')

A delightful little Patio rose with plentiful dark glossy foliage and clusters of cupped, semi-double flowers with slightly wavy petals of a delicate, soft clear pink, borne in profusion throughout summer into autumn. Ideal for containers, including hanging baskets and large window boxes. Height 40cm (16in), spread 60cm (24in).

■ LEFT

'RED ACE' (SYN. 'AMANDA', 'AMRUDA')

One of the most sumptuous reds among the miniature roses, this little bush has a neat, leafy habit and produces clusters of rounded, semi-double, rich crimson blooms from summer to autumn. They are perfect for cutting, and this variety makes fine edging to a border, dramatic massed plantings and a beautiful specimen for containers. Height 30cm (12in), spread 30cm (12in).

■ RIGHT

'RED MEIDILAND' (SYN. 'MEINEBLE', 'ROUGE MEILLANDÉCAR')

A dense, compact ground-cover rose with clusters of relatively large, deep red, single, cupped flowers with white centres and a boss of golden stamens, borne almost continuously from summer to autumn and followed by small red hips. It is suitable for the front of a shrub or mixed border, and is particularly useful for clothing sunny banks or trailing over a retaining wall. Height 75cm (30in), spread 1.5m (5ft).

■ LEFT

'RISE 'N' SHINE'
(SYN. 'GOLDEN MEILLANDINA',
'GOLDEN SUNBLAZE')

A miniature bush rose of neat, compact habit producing clusters of small but well-formed, fully double, urn-shaped, sunny yellow flowers with pointed petals, from summer right through to autumn. Use in containers of all sorts, and as low edging in formal beds and borders. Height 40cm (16in), spread 25cm (10in).

■ RIGHT

'SCARLET MEIDILAND'
(SYN. 'MEIKROTAL')

A ground-cover shrub rose with ample, glossy foliage and large, heavy clusters of many small, cherry-red, rounded, double blooms with golden stamens, produced in abundance from summer onwards; the autumn flushes of flower are notably profuse. It is suitable for the middle ranks of a shrub or mixed border, and for low hedging and containers; it even tolerates light shade. Height 90cm (3ft), spread 1.8m (6ft).

■ LEFT

'SUN HIT' (SYN. 'POULSUN')

A compact Patio rose of upright habit bearing sunny golden-yellow, fully double, urn-shaped blooms with moderately good scent in great profusion from summer to autumn. Bred as a pot-rose, its small stature is ideally suited to containers and window boxes, and it can also be brought into the house when in bloom. Also available as a standard. Height 45cm (18in), spread 45cm (18in).

■ BELOW

'SUSSEX' (SYN. 'POULAV')

A vigorous ground-cover rose producing masses of flowers from early summer to autumn; the fully double, rounded, neatly formed flowers are a soft apricot-pink. Ideal on a sunny bank, at the front of a border and in large planters. Height 45cm (18in), spread 90cm (36in).

■ ABOVE

'SURREY' (SYN. 'KORLANUM', 'SOMMERWIND', 'VENT D'ÉTÉ')

A robust ground-cover rose that looks superb in large containers, in borders or as a specimen. It has a leafy habit, producing dense mounds of foliage and long stems wreathed with abundant clusters of double, cupped, warm-pink flowers from summer to autumn. Height 90cm (3ft), spread 1.2m (4ft).

■ RIGHT

'SWANY' (SYN. 'MEIBURENAC')

A bushy, spreading and very elegant ground-cover rose with plentiful dark green, slightly bronzed, very glossy foliage that acts as a perfect foil to the wreathing clusters of flat, double, pure white flowers. It is suitable for containers – especially charming in a formal courtyard setting – and in mixed borders. Height 90cm (3ft), spread 1.5m (5ft).

■ ABOVE

'SWEET MAGIC' (SYN. 'DICMAGIC')

An attractive, award-winning Patio rose with dense, bright green foliage and full clusters of scented, double, rounded soft apricot-orange and yellow flowers that are borne freely from summer to autumn. A perfect container specimen and ideal for edging. Height 40cm (16in), spread 40cm (16in).

■ RIGHT

'SWEET DREAM' (SYN. 'FRYMINICOT')

A neat, upright Patio rose with moderate scent and a very attractive 'old-fashioned' flower form; a deserving award-winner. The fully double, lightly scented warm apricot-pink flowers are in quartered-rosette form and borne in abundant clusters from summer to autumn. Elegant in containers or as ribbon edging to paths and beds. Height 40cm (16in), spread 35cm (14in).

■ RIGHT

'THE FAIRY'

A sweet Polyantha rose, a deserving award-winner with a good health record, that blooms almost continuously from late summer to autumn. It has a dense, spreading, cushion-like habit, and bears dainty sprays of small, fully double, very pretty rosette-shaped flowers in pale pink. Lovely in a shrub or mixed border and elegant in containers. Height 60cm (2ft), spread 1.2m (4ft).

■ LEFT

'TOP MARKS' (SYN. 'FRYMINISTAR')

A neat, cushion-forming Patio rose with abundant glossy foliage and well-filled clusters of double, rounded, brilliant orange-vermilion flowers from summer to autumn. An award-winning rose, it is suitable for edging borders and bedding, and makes a striking specimen in containers. Height 40cm (16in), spread 45cm (18in).

■ RIGHT

'WARM WELCOME' (SYN. 'CHEWIZZ')

A glossy-leaved miniature climber producing small, semi-double, urn-shaped, bright orange-vermilion flowers freely and almost continuously from summer to autumn. Good for walls in small courtyards or where space is restricted. Height 2.2m (7ft), spread 2.2m (7ft).

■ ABOVE

'WHITE CÉCILE BRÜNNER'

A diminutive Polyantha bush bred at the turn of the century, with plentiful dark green foliage and dainty sprays of sweet-scented, beautifully fully double, urn-shaped white flowers, faintly peach-tinted, borne almost continuously from summer to autumn. Almost thornless, it is ideal for a mixed border or for large urns and other substantial containers. A perfect buttonhole flower. Height 1m (3ft), spread 1m (3ft).

■ ABOVE

'WHITE FLOWER CARPET' (SYN. 'SCHNEEFLOCKE')

A dense, dark-leaved, almost evergreen ground-cover shrub with an excellent health record. Mounds of foliage offset clusters of large, cupped, semi-double white flowers, borne from summer to autumn. Excellent on a sunny bank, as a standard or trailing over a wall. There are red and pink forms too. Height 75cm (30in), spread 1.2m (4ft).

■ LEFT

'WILTSHIRE' (SYN. 'KORMUSE')

A spreading ground-cover shrub that is excellent for banks and planters. The dense glossy foliage is almost obscured by large clusters of lightly scented, rounded, double, deep reddish-pink flowers borne from summer to autumn. Height 60cm (2ft), spread 1.2m (4ft).

The Grower's Guide

This practical section includes advice on choosing the right rose for your garden, as well as step-by-step instructions on how to plant both container-grown and bare-root roses. Once established, roses do not require a lot of work but most do need to be cut back annually. This section shows you how to prune different sorts of roses, and explains the pests and diseases you should look out for during your routine maintenance. There are often easy solutions, especially if the problem is caught early.

■ RIGHT

This well-pruned floribunda rose has plenty of new, vigorous, even growth and an abundance of flowers.

Buying roses

Choosing new roses for the garden is one of the most enjoyable of all gardening activities, for it carries with it the anticipation of many years of pleasure from these generally long-lived shrubs. It is most important to consider the space that you have available and to select a rose variety of a suitable size so that it will not rapidly outgrow the allotted space. Proportion becomes all the more important if you wish to grow roses in containers.

There are several ways to make your selection, all of them pleasurable. You can look online, through gardening books and specialist rose catalogues at leisure by the fireside while you plan your plantings for the following season, or you can visit garden centres to make your selection. But perhaps the best way of selecting roses is to visit gardens in your locality, where they can be observed in growth and flower, so that you can take note of any that attract your attention. Many specialist nurseries have rose gardens attached to the nursery and encourage buyers to visit them during the summer.

Ideally, you should make several visits – this is, after all, no great hardship – so that you can check on their continuity of flowering performance and their overall health and vigour. In any rose collection you will notice individual cultivars that are markedly more free-flowering or healthy and disease-resistant. If any of these roses suit your purpose, you would be well advised to grow them in preference to those that perform less well – good disease-resistance does much to reduce the necessity of repeated applications of chemical pesticides and fungicides.

Once you have decided on a rose that appeals to you and that suits the location and the purpose for which it is to be used, you have to set about finding it. Many garden centres carry a wide range of container-grown roses, and, with luck, the one you want will be in stock. Buying in this way has the advantage of allowing you to check over the plants yourself before purchase and select the most healthy specimen.

■ RIGHT,

Many specialist nurseries have extensive rose gardens to display their wares and to help you make your choice.

If you cannot find the rose you want at a garden centre, you need to look to a specialist supplier, preferably one that is a member of your national Rose Growers' Association. Most national rose societies produce 'who grows what' booklets, which list roses and the nurseries that supply them. Many national horticultural societies also sponsor publications of general plant lists and supplying nurseries. These leaflets are absolutely indispensable when you are trying to track down the lesser known cultivars.

You can buy happily from a reputable nursery, either directly or by mail order, for they strive constantly to produce good, healthy stock and will guarantee that their plants are well grown and true to name. Most nurseries will replace without quibble any plants that you find are unsatisfactory when your order arrives.

Roses are sold either as container-grown or bare-root plants – that is, those that have been lifted from the open ground while dormant and the roots shaken free of soil. Both types eventually make equally good plants, although container-grown roses usually establish more quickly.

■ ABOVE
***R.* 'Cécile Brünner' is a perennial favourite; healthy and floriferous, it is perfect in this elegant container.**

Whichever type of rose you buy, good soil preparation before planting is essential if the rose is to perform well, and will considerably minimize maintenance of the plant later on.

Bare-root plants

Most growers who sell by mail order supply their roses as bare-root plants. They are usually available only between autumn and early spring. Although there may be a delay between ordering your plants and delivery, a huge range is available to you, including rare varieties.

The roses are usually dispatched in specially designed padded envelopes. The roots are wrapped in a polythene bag containing peat or a similar material to keep them moist. You can store the roses unopened for up to six weeks in a dark, cool, frost-free place.

Bare-root roses must be ordered in advance and planted in the autumn or spring.

■ ABOVE
Mail-order companies usually have a large selection of bare-rooted rose varieties.

Container-grown plants

Roses sold in containers are lifted from the field, potted up and grown on. They are available at garden centres throughout the growing season. Garden centres usually prefer to sell plants that are in full growth in containers, but they offer a much smaller choice and only the most popular varieties are likely to be available. Many gardeners find container-grown roses more convenient than bare-root plants, although they are more expensive.

When you are buying a container-grown rose, choose one that is growing evenly, with sturdy, well-spaced stems, and that has a well-balanced appearance. It should be well clothed in ample, healthy foliage that is of good colour. Avoid any plant with sparse or yellowed foliage or one that has evidence of leaf drop, which may indicate that the plant has been starved of nutrients or moisture. Such a rose will not establish well.

If possible, check that it is not pot-bound by sliding the plant from its container so that you can see the root system. The container should be well filled with healthy roots, and the growing medium should be evenly moist – neither dry nor waterlogged.

■ ABOVE
Roses sold in containers are usually in full growth.

If the roots are congested and tightly coiled around the pot, reject it. The roots will probably continue to grow in a spiral, and such plants will establish only slowly, if at all.

Look for signs of disease or pest attack, especially aphids, which generally cluster at the soft shoot tips, and blackspot and rust, which infect the foliage, and reject any plant that is dying back. The presence of a few weed seedlings on the surface of the compost is of no consequence, but a mat of liverworts or mosses suggests that the plant has been in its pot for too long and has exhausted the

nutrients in the compost, or that the plant has been waterlogged.

Although the preferred planting season is between late autumn and early spring, garden centres may have roses in stock throughout much of the growing season, and container-grown roses can be planted at any time of year except when the ground is frozen or waterlogged or during periods of drought in summer.

If you buy during the summer months, the roses will almost certainly be in flower and should be rigorously deadheaded, and pruned where necessary, before planting.

In addition, remember that if you plant in late spring or during the summer months you will need to water the plants thoroughly until they are established, paying particular attention to this during dry weather.

■ ABOVE
If possible, slide a container-grown rose from its container before buying so that you can check that the root system is healthy. The roots should fill the pot but should not be so crowded that they spiral around on themselves.

Soil and fertilizers

■ BELOW
Rosa moyesii, planted among salvias and edged with box, provides a stunning display in late summer.

Roses will tolerate most soil types, except soil that is permanently wet, but the ideal is an easily workable loam, made up of roughly equal parts of sand, silt and clay, that is rich in humus (decayed vegetable matter). Roses are said to prefer heavy clay soils that retain nutrients well, but good results can be achieved on thin, alkaline soil, provided you improve it before planting and mulch the plants annually. Adding organic matter in the form of well-rotted farmyard manure or garden compost improves all soil types, helping to aerate heavy soils and adding bulk and nutrients to light soils. If you have a very heavy soil, working in horticultural grit at the rate of a bucketful per square metre/yard will improve the drainage.

For the best results you will need to feed your roses regularly. Whether you use organic or inorganic fertilizers is a matter of personal choice, but if you use chemical fertilizers you will know exactly how much of the nutrient elements you are applying. Nitrogen (N) stimulates lush, leafy growth, potassium (K) promotes flower production, and phosphorus (P) aids root development. Balanced fertilizers (straights) contain equal amounts of each, but for optimum performance use a commercial rose fertilizer that contains a higher proportion of potassium. Organic gardeners could use pelleted chicken manure instead. Trace elements are also present in the soil, but there is rarely a deficiency and they seldom need to be applied.

Some fertilizers are in powder or granular form, to be forked in around the plant; others are liquid feeds, which are applied as a root drench from a watering can or sprayed on as foliar feed. Foliar feeds are useful if you need to give a rose a boost after an attack of a disease or pest, because the nutrients are immediately available to the plant.

Fork your chosen fertilizer into the soil around the base of the plant when new growth begins in spring. Water in well, then apply a mulch to help retain moisture. On repeat-flowering roses, you should feed again in mid-summer, immediately after deadheading, but do not feed again after this, because you will encourage lush growth that will not have time to ripen fully before winter. Forking in a handful of bonemeal around the base of the plant in autumn, however, will promote strong root growth. Even though top growth has ceased, roots continue to grow.

Soil improvers

Farmyard manure
An excellent soil improver, although you must ensure that it the farmyard manure is well rotted or it may take nitrogen out of the soil as it breaks down. Its nutrient quotient can be low relative to its bulk. Chicken and pigeon manure is high in nitrogen.

Peat
A light and pleasant to handle material. Peat is inert and does not provide any additional nutrients. Nowadays, extensive use of peat is discouraged and many gardeners prefer to avoid its use because peat is not a renewable resource. Removing peat damages the environment.

Garden compost
The best of all soil improvers, garden compost is both friable in texture and high in nutrients. It also has the advantage of being free. It is, however, difficult to make sufficient quantities of compost to satisfy all your gardening needs. Avoid the use of diseased material as compost.

■ RIGHT
By the end of its first season a newly planted rose should have made good growth and may even flower.

Grit
Although it is often used to improve the drainage of very heavy clay soils, grit is inert and does not contain any nutrients. Grit can be used as a mulch and as a top-dressing for plants in containers.

Leaf mould
A superb soil improver, leaf mould is light in texture and virtually weed-free. It is made by allowing fallen leaves (which must be disease-free) to break down and usually takes about two years to produce.

Spent mushroom compost
Available from commercial producers, spent mushroom compost is an excellent material, fertile and usually weed free. However, it tends to be chalky and should not be added to soils that are already very alkaline.

Fertilizers

Bonemeal
An organic fertilizer, high in phosphorus, which breaks down slowly in the soil. Fork bonemeal into the soil on planting and use it as a top-dressing in autumn. When handling bonemeal, always wear rubber gloves and a mask.

Rose fertilizer
Proprietary rose fertilizers are inorganic and contain all the major elements with a high proportion of potassium. Apply at the start of the growing season and, if necessary, in summer after the first flush of flowers to build up the plant's resources for later flowering.

Growmore
A balanced (straight), inorganic fertilizer that contains all the major elements in equal proportions. Use it at the start of the growing season to give roses a boost. Growmore should be used in place of, not as well as, any other fertilizer.

Pelleted chicken manure
This organic fertilizer is becoming increasingly popular. It is higher in potassium than raw manure.

Planting in open ground

Most roses grow best in full sun but with some protection from wind. Very exposed sites are suitable only for the tough rugosas, which will also tolerate some degree of shade, although flowering is less profuse. A few roses tolerate dappled shade, although growth and flowering will be less vigorous. No rose will perform well in deep shade.

Good air circulation around the plants is important and lessens the likelihood of mildew and other fungal diseases. Consider the spread of the full-grown rose before you plant. Even roses intended to make a hedge should be placed at least 1m/3ft apart. Planting too close to other shrubs will also limit the moisture and nutrients available to both plants.

Before planting, the site should be prepared thoroughly by digging and forking it over to break up and aerate the soil. Remove any large stones you come across. Organic matter greatly improves the texture of all soil, opening up heavy soil that clogs by binding it into crumbs, while aiding water retention on light, sandy ground. Fork in garden compost or farmyard manure at the rate of about one bucketful per square metre/yard.

Take great care to completely remove all trace of weeds, especially perennial weeds such as couch grass and ground elder. Weeds are much easier to eradicate before the rose is planted, as the roots of the two plants quickly become entangled.

Bare-root roses should be planted as soon after receipt as possible, preferably during a mild spell. If the ground is unworkable, because it is frozen or waterlogged, the rose can be stored unopened for up to six weeks in a cool, dark, frost-free place. When you are ready to plant, remove the packaging and cut back any damaged

PLANTING A BARE-ROOT ROSE

1 Dig a hole large enough to take the roots when they are spread out and deep enough not to bend them. Incorporate garden compost or well-rotted manure in the base if not already added to the soil when the bed was prepared.

2 Work a handful of bonemeal into the planting hole (wear gloves), then spread out the roots evenly, with the plant placed centrally. If the roots grow in just one direction, do not bend them, but plant the rose to one side of the hole.

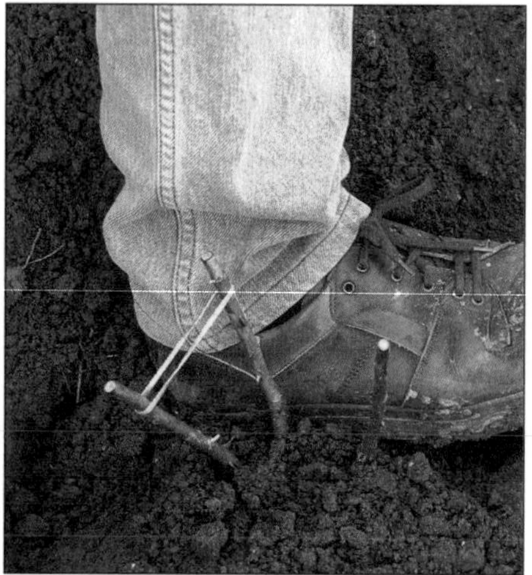

3 Trickle the soil between the roots, shaking the plant occasionally as the hole is filled to settle the soil. Tread around the base of the plant to firm the soil, and make sure the budding is completely covered to prevent suckers.

or twiggy growth. Lightly trim the root, then soak the rose for about an hour in a bucket of water.

Container-grown roses can be planted at any time of year, except when the ground is frozen, waterlogged or during periods of drought. If you cannot plant immediately, keep the rose in a sheltered place and water regularly.

It is a complete myth that roses cannot be grown in soil where roses have previously been grown. It is now believed that roses enjoy a relationship with beneficial underground fungi that attach themselves to the roots and facilitate the up-take of water – and hence nutrients – from the soil. The fungi belong to a group known as mycorrhizal fungi, and they are now available commercially in sachets for adding to planting holes. They are particularly useful for helping roses establish on poor quality or virgin soils, and on soils from which older roses have been removed.

Once planted, a rose should be watered regularly until it is established. Adding a top-dressing such as chipped bark will help keep water evaporation to a minimum, and also help in the suppression of weeds.

Roses planted in the spring should quickly put forward new shoots, and may flower the following year.

PLANTING A CONTAINER-GROWN ROSE

1 Excavate a hole approximately twice the width of the container and a little deeper. Break up the soil in the bottom with a fork, incorporating humus-forming material, such as garden compost or well-rotted manure, if this has not already been done in the general preparation of the bed.

2 Remove the rose from its pot. Gently tease out some of the roots from around the edge to encourage them to grow out into the surrounding soil, then position the rootball in the hole. Lay a cane across the hole to check the depth, adding or removing soil as necessary.

3 The graft union (that point where the rose was budded on to its rootstock) should be about 2.5cm/1in below the level of the surrounding bed. Backfill with soil and firm in with your foot to ensure there are no large air pockets where the roots will dry out.

4 If you are planting in spring or early summer, apply a general garden fertilizer or one formulated for roses, and fork it in lightly. Water well, then mulch with more organic material, such as garden compost or chipped bark, to reduce water evaporation and suppress weeds.

Planting climbing roses

Climbing roses are planted like bush roses, depending on whether they are bare-root or container grown. However, all will need some form of support, whether this be a free-standing or wall mounted trellis, a system of wires, or a host plant, usually a tree.

Rose stems need to be tied in as they grow since they are not self-supporting, though thorny stemmed roses will hook themselves into a tree's bark once established.

CLIMBING ROSES THAT WILL TOLERATE SOME SHADE

- 'Albéric Barbier'
- 'American Pillar'
- 'Blush Rambler'
- 'Climbing Cécile Brünner'
- 'Crimson Descant'
- 'Félicité Perpétue'
- 'Golden Showers'
- 'Goldfinch'
- 'Maigold'
- 'Madame Alfred Carrière'
- 'Mermaid'
- 'New Dawn'
- 'Paul's Scarlet Climber'
- 'Phyllis Bide'
- 'Veilchenblau'

USING VINE EYES

■ ABOVE
Flat vine eyes are suitable for brick and stone walls, and can be hammered straight in. They are less good for wooden fences.

■ ABOVE
Screw-in vine eyes can be used on timber or brick. A wall plug is inserted into the hole, and the eye is screwed into the plug.

Making a system of wires

To grow a rose against a wall, you must first fix either a trellis or system of wires to the wall. Vine eyes (which hold stretched wires to which rose stems are tied) are both unobtrusive and flexible. They offer by far the best means of support to climbing roses.

Vine eyes are of two types, screw in (to be used in conjunction with wall plugs) and hammer in (for use in masonry). The screw in type normally close with a ring, while the hammer-in vine eyes are flat and roughly triangular. Both are available in a number of sizes.

Space the vine eyes about 1m/3ft apart horizontally and 30cm/12in vertically, then thread plastic-coated wire between them to make horizontal courses. Tie the rose stems to the wires with horticultural twine or wire ties. You will probably need to tighten the wires occasionally. Once the rose is established the wires are scarcely visible. You can add further wires as the plant grows.

Walls cast a rain shadow: the soil at the foot of the wall does not become as wet during showers as soil in the open border, so plant the rose at least 45cm/18in away from the wall to ensure that the roots receive adequate moisture..

Planting through a tree

If you wish to grow a rose through a tree, you must first make sure that you have compatible candidates. Neither plant should compete unduly for moisture or nutrients or both will suffer. In addition the tree must be strong enough to bear the considerable weight of a full-grown rose. Conifers and apple trees are often suitable to grow roses through. The tree should be neither too young nor too old. A young tree may be smothered by the vigorous rose, while the additional burden of a climber may be too much for an older, weaker tree during winter storms.

VIGOROUS ROSES SUITABLE FOR GROWING THROUGH TREES

'Albéric Barbier'	'Félicité Perpétue'
'Albertine'	*R. filipes* 'Kiftsgate'
'Alister Stella Gray'	'Madame Alfred Carrière'
'American Pillar'	*R. mulliganii*
'Blush Rambler'	'Paul's Himalayan Musk'
'Bobbie James'	'Rambling Rector'
'Climbing Cécile Brünner'	'Seagull'
'Complicata'	'Wedding Day'
'Excelsa'	

The rose should be planted at least 1m/3ft from the tree trunk. Pay particular attention to soil preparation, adding plenty of garden compost or farmyard manure.

Position the rose on the side of the prevailing wind so that it will blow the stems of the climber into the tree as the rose grows. Water well until the rose becomes established.

PLANTING A CLIMBING ROSE AGAINST A TREE

1 Dig a hole about 1m/3ft across and 45cm/18in deep. It should be 1m/3ft from the base of the tree.

2 Add organic matter, then fork in bonemeal at the base of the hole, following the manufacturer's instructions.

3 Check the depth of the hole, then plant the rose, angling the top growth towards the tree trunk.

4 Insert canes by the rose, then tie these to the tree. Tie the stems of the rose to the canes.

Using a trellis

A trellis can be made of wood, plastic or some other synthetic material. The sturdiest types are best, since most climbing roses are vigorous plants that can pull down a flimsy structure. If you opt for a wood trellis make sure that it has been pressure-treated with preservative so that it will not rot. There are now a wide choice of colours available to stain wood if the trellis is not to your liking, but make sure that any stain you use is not toxic to plants. Heavy duty trellis is available at builder's merchants as well as garden centres.

Large trellis panels can be used in conjunction with fence panels or on their own to make a free standing screen. In both cases they should be nailed to timber uprights that are embedded in the ground, either in concrete or in special metal supports.

Any trellis placed against a wall should be mounted on battens to ensure adequate air circulation between the plant and the wall. This will minimize the risk of airborne fungal diseases such as mildew. Battens also make it possible to remove the rose from the wall if you need to paint or repair the wall at a later date. Remember that the battens should also be treated with a plant-friendly wood preservative.

STARTING A TRELLIS ROSE

1 Decide on the best position for the trellis on the wall and drill holes at suitable intervals to take the battens. Tap in plugs to take the screws.

2 Screw the battens to the wall using rust-proof screws.

3 Check the position of the trellis and fix it firmly to the battens.

4 Fork over the planting area, thoroughly working in organic matter such as spent mushroom compost.

5 Dig a hole at least 45cm/18in from the wall. Fork in a handful of bonemeal at the bottom of the hole.

6 Check the planting depth. You should aim to cover the graft union. Plant the rose so that it is just below the level of the soil.

7 Remove the rose from its pot and tease out some of the roots. This will help them grow quickly into the surrounding soil and let the rose become established.

8 Position the rose in the hole, angling the top growth towards the wall and fanning out the roots away from the wall. Backfill with soil.

9 Firm the rose in with your feet to eliminate any pockets of air around the roots. Gently pull on the stem to check that the rose is securely planted.

10 Cut back any dead or damaged growth to healthy wood, but leave longer, healthy stems unpruned. Remove any faded flowers.

11 If the stems are long enough, fan them out horizontally and tie them loosely to the trellis. Water well. If you are planting in spring, fork in some fertilizer.

12 Correctly planted, the rose should quickly establish and will soon produce vigorous new shoots that can be trained to the trellis.

Planting a standard rose

Standard roses lend height to rose beds and act as focal points, but they can be used just as effectively in summer bedding schemes and as container plants on the patio.

Roses grown as standards inevitably become focal points in a way that an individual bush rose seldom can. Not only are they raised above most of the other roses, they have an architectural shape that simply demands attention. For that reason a single specimen in the centre of a formal flower bed is often the focal point, and when planted in a rose bed a single standard rose can compete with perhaps dozens of lower growing large-flowered or cluster-flowered roses in visual terms.

Be cautious, however, when planting standards among other roses. Standards come in different heights, and the impact will be lost if a small standard is planted among tall bush roses.

Standards are not specific varieties, but ordinary bush roses budded on to a long stem, which makes it possible to plant bush and standard forms of the same variety – for example, standard and bush forms of 'Iceberg' in an all-white bed. For a less subtle or more dazzling effect, choose a contrasting colour.

Weeping standards are usually varieties of ramblers. The stems cascade and are sometimes trained over an umbrella-shaped frame, although many 'experts' do not approve of them and consider that the stems look better if allowed to cascade naturally.

Whichever method you choose, a weeping standard will produce a curtain of colour, with stems that often cascade to ground level. Ground-cover roses – 'Grouse' (syn. 'Immensee', 'Korimro') and 'Nozomi' (syn. 'Heideröslein'), for example – are used to produce weeping standards, but even shrub roses with arching stems – 'Ballerina' and *R. xanthina* 'Canary Bird', for instance – can be obtained in this form.

Weeping roses almost always look best as specimen plants in a lawn, where their symmetry and beauty can be fully appreciated.

Patio standards are usually dwarf cluster-flowered roses on stems about 75cm/2½ft tall, and these look perfect by the front door in a light porch, as well as on the patio.

■ RIGHT

An eye-catching individual standard rose adds style and contrast when planted in front of a formal dark hedge.

HOW TALL?

Standards vary in height. Although different growers may use slightly different terminology and sizes, this chart gives typical stem heights (the actual head may increase the total height):

Miniature standard – 45cm/18in
Half-standard – 75cm/2½ft
Patio standard – 75cm/2½ft
Full standard – 1m/3ft
Weeping standard – 1.2–1.5m/4–5ft

Planting standard roses is slightly more involved than planting an ordinary container-grown rose.

One of the most important aspects to consider before you decide the final position of the rose, is the amount of protection that is available. A reasonably sheltered site is essential because standard roses are top heavy and are easily blown over or damaged by strong winds. If it is planted properly, however, with the roots undamaged by the stake, the rose will flourish.

Water well throughout the first growing season until the rose is established. Remember to check the main stem occasionally for suckers.

PLANTING A CONTAINER-GROWN STANDARD ROSE

1 Choose a well-protected site, then dig a hole that is twice the depth and twice the width of the container. Fork in bonemeal and garden compost, well-rotted farmyard manure or leaf mould into the base of the hole.

2 Check the planting depth. The surface of the surrounding soil should be level with the soil in the container. If you are planting a bare-root standard, look for the soil mark on the stem, which indicates the level of planting in the nursery.

3 Position the rose in the centre of the hole, then drive in a stake that is just off-centre, avoiding the roots. The stake should come to just below the head of the rose.

4 Slide the rose from its container and gently tease out the roots with a hand fork.

5 Set the rose in position and backfill the hole with soil. Firm in well.

6 Use ties to fasten the stem of the rose to the stake. Water the rose thoroughly.

Planting in containers

Some roses will do well in containers, but they require careful planting to get them off to a good start and to provide the conditions that will sustain them in future years.

Old roses can be successfully grown in containers, as long as the container is large enough to accommodate the rose's root run. The rose will probably be in the container for several years, so it is worth spending time on the planting. Many modern roses, too, are suitable for growing in containers. All the miniature and patio roses are obvious candidates, but there are other shorter growing and less vigorous varieties that will lend themselves perfectly to being grown in a container. Check the expected height and spread of the rose and choose a container to suit.

There is a huge number of different styles of container to choose from, ranging from the very modern to reproductions of classic designs. Chose a container whose colour and style fits with both your garden and the rose you intend to grow.

If you can, use a heavy stone or unglazed terracotta container. They are water- and air-permeable, thus reducing the risk of waterlogging, while also providing good ballast to prevent the container from blowing over during strong winds. For a more rustic look, a half-barrel would make a less expensive alternative.

■ ABOVE

Ground-cover roses are versatile plants. They are ideal for raised beds, patios and rock gardens, as well as being effective container plants.

Plastic pots are lighter and therefore less stable, especially for a large plant, but could be used for one of the dainty tea or China roses. Plastic pots are usually suitable for roses grown under glass, where wind is not a problem.

For larger roses plastic pots are really only suitable where there is no alternative, such as on a balcony or roof garden. They tend to become waterlogged and often overheat in summer. Plastic containers do have the advantage that they do not lose water through evaporation through the sides, as unglazed terracotta pots do, and therefore need watering less often. If you have a balcony or roof garden you must secure the container to a wall or railings.

Decide on the final position of the container before you begin planting, because it will be very heavy to move when it is finished. Adding a layer of stones or gravel in the base of the pot adds greatly to the weight of the container, but it is important both for drainage and to counterbalance the weight of the fully grown rose: a top-heavy container is at a greater risk of being blown over in storms.

Roses in containers do best in soil-based composts (soil mixes), preferably a John Innes No. 3, which have a number of advantages over soil-less mixes. If they are allowed to dry out, soil-based composts (soil mixes) are easier to re-wet. They also tend to have a higher nutrient quotient. If weight is a consideration, you can still achieve good results with soil-less composts, provided you feed and water the plants regularly.

To maintain vigour in subsequent years, top-dress with bonemeal or work in rose fertilizer at the rate recommended by the manufacturer at the time of planting. Supplementary feeding will also be necessary in the future. Use a proprietary rose fertilizer or a liquid feed or pelleted fertilizer for plants in containers.

All roses in containers – but especially those in hanging baskets – need regular watering. You will need to water at least once, and probably twice, a day at the height of summer. Adding water-retaining granules to the compost when you are planting can help to overcome the problem.

Plants in containers are vulnerable to sudden changes in temperature. The roots can bake in summer if they are standing on a hard, concrete surface that reflects heat, so some shade from the hot midday sun may be necessary.

In winter the compost can freeze solid. Either move pots into a sheltered spot or wrap them loosely in hessian (burlap) or bubble-wrap.

Remember, too, to keep the surface of the compost weed free. Stone chippings, fine gravel or chipped bark can be added to help suppress their growth. Not only will weeds detract from the appearance of the rose, they will compete with it for moisture and nutrients.

MODERN ROSES SUITABLE FOR GROWING IN A CONTAINER

- 'Anisley Dickson'
- 'Amber Queen'
- 'Arthur Bell'
- 'Blue Moon'
- 'Double Delight'
- 'Elizabeth Harkness'
- 'Ingrid Bergman'
- 'King's Ransom'
- 'Margaret Merril'
- 'Precious Platinum'
- 'Princess Michael of Kent'
- 'Sexy Rexy'
- 'Southampton'
- 'Tango'

■ RIGHT

Group small roses in containers of different sizes and shapes to create an attractive feature near the front door, in a courtyard or to decorate a patio.

Planting a rose in a container

1 Cover the base of a large pot or half-barrel with stones or fill one-third full of gravel to provide stability. Use a loam-based soil mix or equal quantities of loam-based potting mix and garden compost to fill the pot deep enough to support the root ball. Work in a handful of bonemeal.

2 Check the planting depth while the rose is still in its pot. There should be a gap of about 2.5cm/1in between the rim of the container and the top surface of the soil mix to allow for watering.

3 Remove the rose from its pot and gently tease out the roots with your fingers or a hand fork. This will help the plant to become established more quickly.

4 Backfill with more soil mix and firm in with your hands to remove pockets of air. Ensure that the graft union between the top growth and rootstock is covered.

5 Water the plant thoroughly with a fine rose attached to a watering can or hosepipe.

6 Top-dress with chipped bark, stone chippings or fine gravel to keep the roots cool, prevent excess evaporation and improve the appearance of the container.

Planting in a hanging basket

■ ABOVE
As a rose in a hanging basket grows, it will disguise most of the basket and moss.

Choose a hanging basket to suit the size of the rose. A 35–40cm/14–16in basket will hold three or four ground-cover roses, but you can use smaller baskets for single plantings.

To conserve water, line the basket with sphagnum moss and then insert a plastic liner, with drainage holes pierced in it. As long as you remember to feed the established plants regularly, the lighter weight of peat-based growing mixes and composts is more easily managed in a hanging basket.

Hang the planted basket in place before watering thoroughly. A large basket will be too heavy to lift safely when it has been well watered. If you want to create a mixed planting with annuals or small trailing perennials, plant these around the base of the rose before watering.

Once planted, the basket may be stored in a sheltered place outdoors or, if planted in late winter, in a cold greenhouse until spring to allow the plants to become well established before being exposed to the elements.

Because hanging baskets are more exposed to wind, they dry out more rapidly than other containers, and are likely to need watering every day in warm weather. Place them where water is easily accessible, therefore. Most garden centres stock pump-action, high-level watering devices that will make the task easier.

PLANTING A ROSE IN A HANGING BASKET

1 Line the hanging basket with a layer of sphagnum moss, which looks attractive and can also hold many times its own weight of water.

2 To conserve even more moisture, add a second lining of black plastic into which a number of holes have been pierced to permit free drainage.

3 Add a layer of the potting medium of your choice, insert the plant and backfill firmly with more soil mix. Hang up the basket and water thoroughly.

Planting a climbing rose in a container

Although most climbing roses are unsuitable for growing in containers, there are several modern hybrids that make excellent plants for containers. All miniature climbing roses can be used for this purpose, and are the ideal plants to liven up a patio, terrace or roof garden. Miniature roses bear clusters of small, usually double flowers similar to those of true miniature and patio roses. They make plants no more than 2.1m/7ft high when grown in the open border, and they are unlikely to exceed 1.5m/5ft in height when grown in a container. A climbing rose in a container can be pruned and trained in the same way as a climbing rose in the garden, but for optimum performance, pay more attention to watering and feeding. Water freely during the growing season. At the height of summer you will need to water at least once, possibly even twice, a day. Feed with a specially formulated rose fertilizer at the start of the season to encourage flower production, and then again after the first flush of flowers. For added vigour, spray the plant regularly with a foliar feed.

Roses should not be fed after mid-summer, since this promotes sappy growth that will not ripen fully before winter and will therefore be susceptible to frost damage and may be liable to disease.

PLANTING A ROSE IN A CONTAINER

1 Cover drainage holes at the base of the container with stones or gravel to improve the drainage. It will also improve stability. Begin to fill the container with compost (soil mix).

2 Check the planting depth by standing the rose in its container on the compost. Make sure that the graft union is covered with compost and leave a gap of about 2.5cm/1in below the rim of the container to allow for watering.

3 Ease the rose out of its container and tease out the roots with a hand fork so that they grow away quickly.

4 Set the rose in position in the centre of the container and begin to backfill with the growing medium of your choice.

5 Once the correct level has been reached, firm the compost with your hands and water the rose well.

6 Insert canes or bamboo around the edge of the container, pushing them down to the base for maximum stability. An odd number of canes looks best.

7 Tie the tops of the canes together securely to create a wigwam over the container. Alternatively, use a proprietary wigwam support.

8 Run wires or string around the canes at intervals of about 20cm/8in, either as separate rounds or in a continuous spiral. As the rose grows, tie the stems in with wire ties or horticultural string.

9 To provide winter interest when the rose is not in bloom, plant winter pansies or underplant with ivies and a selection of dwarf spring bulbs for welcome spring colour.

SUITABLE CLIMBING AND RAMBLING ROSES FOR CONTAINERS

- 'Casino'
- 'Céline Forestier'
- 'Climbing Orange Sunblaze'
- 'Dublin Bay'
- 'Golden Showers'
- 'Good as Gold'
- 'Laura Ford'
- 'Maigold'
- 'Nice Day'
- 'Phyllis Bide'
- 'Swan Lake'
- 'Warm Welcome'
- 'White Cockade'

Climbing roses in a container can be grown in two ways. They can be trained against a wall to make a spectacular display, or grown up canes set in the container for a free-standing feature.

To train a climber against a wall, first attach a trellis to the wall. The container the plant is in should be considered. Halved half-barrels made of wood are particularly suitable for the purpose because they have flat backs and can be stood directly against the wall. Alternatively, a rose trained on a wigwam of canes can be moved around at will. It can feature prominently when in bloom, and moved elsewhere in the winter.

Whichever method you choose, select a container that is large enough to allow a good root run. Stability is an important factor, so the container should be heavy enough to support the top growth, which is likely to be substantial once the rose is mature. Light plastic containers are not generally suitable. A heavy, loam-based, high-fertility compost (soil mix) is best. Peat or coir-based composts are suitable, although they are difficult to re-wet if they dry out.

Alternative planting methods

Although all old roses make excellent border plants, blending easily with a range of other flowers, there are a few that may be grown in other ways, often to their advantage.

Pegging down

Some old roses (hybrid perpetuals, most of the bourbons and some modern shrub roses among them) produce a quantity of vigorous but flexible stems from near the base of the plant after flowering. You can take advantage of this habit to enhance the next year's flowering display. Such stems tend to grow upright, then arch over, and will flower only at their tips, but by bringing them down virtually to the horizontal you will encourage them to produce more flowering laterals, particularly on the curve, where growth hormones will accumulate. Using this technique you can train the plant as a short climber, or create a spectacular flowering 'table', a technique usually called 'pegging down'. For a crinoline-like mound of flowers, cut lengths of hazel, or some other flexible wood, insert one end on the ground near the base of the rose, then bend it into a hoop. Tie the rose stems to this as they grow.

■ ABOVE
To peg down a rose, bring a flexible, but vigorous shoot down to as near ground level as possible. Peg it to the soil with lengths of strong wire bent over into hairpin shapes.

■ ABOVE
The shrub rose 'Chianti' has been tied to horizontal wires, which are pinned to stakes about 30cm/12in high. Notice how flowering laterals have been produced all along the length of the stem.

Wall training

If you live in an area with cold winters, you can grow some of the Chinas that will withstand only a few degrees of frost against a warm wall. In summer the extra heat reflected by the wall will help to ripen the stems so that they are better able to withstand low temperatures. Tie them to a trellis or horizontal wires, training vigorous stems as near to the horizontal as possible. Treated in this way a China will grow to twice the height it would have achieved in the open, although its display won't be as spectacular as that of a true climber.

Summer-flowering hedge

Shrub and bush roses make an attractive summer-flowering hedge, although, because they are not evergreen, they do not make a permanent barrier. All the rugosa roses are suitable for this purpose, as are some roses from the other groups. Plant the roses about 1m/3ft apart –

more if they have a wide spread. Hybrid musks, which have a spread that exceeds their height, are best tied to horizontal wires. Most hedges are pruned in summer after flowering by shearing them back to the desired height, but pruning a rugosa hedge then would deprive you of the ornamental hips, so do no more than tidy up the plants in late winter.

■ ABOVE
This Bourbon rose 'Blairii Number Two' has been trained on a pyramid.

■ RIGHT
The spread of this alba rose has been restricted by tying the stems to upright bamboo canes.

Pruning

Pruning a rose refreshes the plant and maintains an open, vase-shaped habit. It also promotes free air circulation through the plant, minimizing the risk of mildew and other fungal diseases. There are no hard and fast rules for pruning: be guided by your own judgement and by the way the rose is growing. Very vigorous roses often achieve their true potential only when left mostly to their own devices. Conversely, some weak-growing roses benefit from regular hard pruning.

Bear in mind a few basic principles. Pruning always stimulates vigorous new growth, which arises from the growth bud nearest to the cut. To promote even, balanced growth, prune straggly, weak stems hard but trim vigorous stems only lightly. If in doubt, prune lightly. You can always prune again later. Roses are, on the whole, forgiving plants. Provided you water, feed and mulch well after pruning you are unlikely to do any lasting harm to the plant, no matter what pruning policy you follow.

Tools

Secateurs (pruners) are suitable for most rose pruning, but you may need loppers (long-handled pruners) or a pruning saw to cut through the thick stems of older plants. Always wear gloves to protect your hands.

Use well-maintained tools with clean, sharp blades. Blunt blades will tear and snag the wood, providing an entry point for disease. After use, clean the blades with an oily rag.

Timing

When you prune your roses is a matter of judgement, depending to some extent on the local climate. In principle, you can prune at any time when the rose is dormant, from late autumn to late winter. In many areas, however, the climate is unpredictable and an early prune – after a warm, wet spell towards the end of winter, for example – can result in a rush of sappy growth that will be damaged by an unexpected late, hard frost. The damage is seldom lasting, but growth will be checked, and you will have to prune again to remove the frosted stems. Where winters are harsh, therefore, delay pruning until early spring. You can also prune late to delay flowering. If the rose is in a container, you can prune as soon as the days begin to lengthen, bringing the plant under glass for early flowers (known as forcing). Commercial growers who exhibit at spring horticultural shows regularly force their plants in this way. Extra heat and light may also be necessary.

■ RIGHT (CLOCKWISE FROM TOP LEFT)
Bypass secateurs (pruning shears), anvil secateurs (pruning shears) and long-handled pruners (loppers or lopping shears) are all useful garden tools.

Renovation

Very old, neglected roses that have accumulated a quantity of unproductive wood can be given a new lease of life by hard pruning.

In late winter or early spring, cut the oldest, thickest stems back to ground level. Shorten the remainder to within 15–30cm/6–12in of the ground. Feed the plant well, water and mulch. New growth will be vigorous, but it is likely to be a year or two before the flowering capacity is fully restored. However, if the rose does not make good growth during the season following renovation, it is beyond salvation.

Making the cuts

Growth buds lie alternately on rose stems. Because the new growth will arise from the bud nearest the cut, prune to a bud that faces in the direction you want the new shoot to grow. Cut just above the bud, angling away from the emerging growth. Remove all diseased, damaged or dead wood, and also any stems that cross or are badly placed. On newly planted roses, cut back the remaining stems lightly to stimulate fresh growth. On established plants, cut back to ground level any old, woody, unproductive stems. If the rose is weak-growing, cut back the remaining stems by up to two-thirds. On vigorous roses, trim back lightly. A selective approach is often best, whereby you remove some stems, shorten others by a third or more, and leave the remainder unpruned or lightly trimmed.

■ ABOVE
Correct pruning cuts. The clean cut, made just above the bud, has been angled away from it. Rain will run off, away from the bud, rather than in to it, where the water may collect and cause rotting.

■ ABOVE
Two incorrect pruning cuts. The stem on the left has been cut too far away from the emerging bud, while the one on the right has been cut too close and the bud has been damaged.

■ RIGHT
In a confined space, train the main stems of a vigorous climbing rose in an S-shape.

Old roses

Most old roses are best left to develop to their true potential with minimal pruning, and the annual, rigorous prune demanded by modern roses is not necessary. However, check plants early in the spring because some pruning may be beneficial. For the general well-being of the plant you should remove any dead, diseased or damaged material and also cut back any branches that cross and rub against each other. Left unpruned, these may damage each other's bark and produce an entry point for disease. Pruning also helps to to create the right shape. Roses should have an open framework, so cut just above an outward-facing bud. A plant with congested growth will not flower well and is susceptible to disease.

It is easiest to prune roses in early spring, when the branches are still relatively bare. You will be able to identify which wood needs to be removed and gain easier access to the base of the plant.

Roses should also be trimmed in mid-summer, immediately after flowering. On roses that flower only once, trimming makes room for strong new growth that will flower freely the following year. On roses that flower again later in season, it encourages a better second crop. During the summer pruning examine the rose carefully and trim back any particulary vigorous shoots which would whip about in winter storms and may lead to wind-rock (loosening of the roots).

Summer pruning should not be carried out on roses which are grown for their ornamental hips as well as for their flowers, such as *R. moyesii*. In general, however, removing the spent flowers improves the overall appearance of the plant.

Gallicas tend to produce a mass of twiggy shoots, which can become congested. Thin the shoots periodically throughout the summer. This will minimize the risk of disease by improving air circulation.

Modern roses

For large-flowered and cluster-flowered roses, autumn and spring pruning both have their advocates. A good compromise is to shorten the height of very tall varieties by about half in autumn, to reduce wind resistance that would cause wind-rock damage by loosening the roots. This is unnecessary with compact varieties.

Most people prefer to prune their roses in early spring, when new growth is beginning but before the leaves start to expand. Pruning at this time of year allows you to select accurately which stems to cut and gives you fairly easy access to the plant to prune.

Although the bushes will look less even in growth, it is possible to extend the year's flowering season a little by leaving some shoots unpruned. These should flower earlier, followed by the pruned shoots. If this method is adopted, be sure to cut back the unpruned shoots the following year. Do not leave any shoots unpruned for more than two consecutive years.

■ LEFT

When you prune you are aiming to create a balanced, open framework that allows good air circulation.

Climbing roses

Climbers need no pruning in their first two or three growing seasons, other than to remove weak, twiggy growth and dead or damaged wood.

In the first few years after planting, keep pruning to a minimum to build up the main framework of stems. This is particularly important on sports of bush roses, such as 'Climbing Blue Moon', which can revert to the bush form if cut back too hard.

Once it is established, a climbing rose should be pruned in early spring. Remove dead, diseased and damaged wood and any weak, spindly shoots. Shorten flowered shoots by two-thirds of their length, cutting to an outward facing bud. If the rose is slow to branch, prune the tips of main shoots by about 5cm/2in, back to a strong bud.

On older plants, if there is adequate new growth, cut back to the base all old main stems that have thickened and are less productive. This should stimulate new replacement shoots that can be tied in to their support when still young and flexible. Any gaps in the cover can be filled in this way, taking advantage of the resulting strong flowering.

■ LEFT
Judicious pruning is essential to maintain a healthy plant and a good display of flowers.

Miniature roses

Ground-cover roses need little pruning on planting, other than to remove dead, damaged, diseased or weak growth. Miniature, patio and polyantha roses are cut back hard on planting, to 7.5–15cm/3–6in above ground level for patio and polyantha roses and to 5–7.5cm/2–3in for miniatures. Cut back each strong shoot to a healthy, outward-facing bud. Remove completely weak or spindly shoots and any that are damaged or dead.

Once established, trailing ground-cover roses need pruning only to keep them within bounds. Cut back over-long shoots to an upward-facing bud. Do this for once-flowering roses after flowering and for repeat-flowering roses during dormancy in early spring. For the shrubby ground-cover roses, prune back the tips of over-long stems lightly and, if the bush is overcrowded, shorten side shoots to two or three buds from their base.

Prune established miniature, patio and polyantha roses in early spring. Remove dead, weak and unhealthy growth, then take out any stems that cross each other or the centre of the bush by cutting back to their point of origin. This is often sufficient to maintain good flowering, but if the rose has not thrived in the previous season, shorten the remaining shoots by up to two-thirds of their length, cutting back to a strong, outward-facing bud.

Pruning old roses

SPRING PRUNING FOR OLD ROSES

1 In early spring cut out all dead growth, going back to the base of the plant if necessary. At the same time, remove any crossing stems that rub against each other.

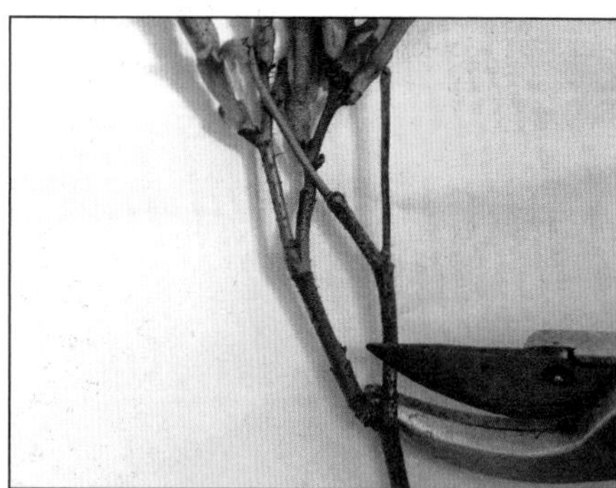

2 Cut back any other dead wood as far as live material.

3 Shorten laterals by between one-third and half their length if necessary. Cut back to a strong bud facing in the direction you want the stem to grow. Shorten any badly placed stems by one-third to a half.

Old roses generally flower on wood that is two years old or more. They need only very light pruning in early spring to tidy up their shape and to remove any dead or diseased stems that could cause problems later.

After spring pruning, apply a fertilizer to the rose. Water it well, and then mulch with well-rotted farmyard manure, bark chippings or garden compost. Feed the roses again after deadheading in the summer.

Old roses which are not performing well can sometimes be rescued by severe pruning. Cut back the oldest stems to ground level and others to within 15–30cm/6–12in of the ground. There will be plenty of strong growth in the following year, with flowers the year after that.

AN EASIER WAY TO PRUNE MODERN ROSES

Pruning a large rose bed, a rose hedge or a border of roses can seem a daunting and time-consuming task, and simply going over the rose bed with a powered hedge-trimmer (shears) is an appealing option. Traditionalist rose-growers will find the suggestion horrifying, but trials with the 'rough and ready' method have shown that both large-flowered (hybrid tea) roses and cluster-flowered (floribunda) roses can actually produce better displays than when pruned conventionally. Established roses are surprisingly resilient and this crude method of pruning can be extremely successful.

There are some drawbacks, however. It is harder to monitor the roses individually, and they may become congested at the centre with a larger amount of dead wood. A congested rose bush, where air cannot circulate freely, traps moisture and thus increases the likelihood of fungi and diseases.

For a general garden display, however, using a powered hedge-trimmer is well worth considering, especially if you keep an eye open for dead or diseased shoots to prune out at the same time.

Although a powered hedge-trimmer will save time, you can use secateurs in the same way. Simply top the shoots at the required level.

Pruning shrub roses

In pruning terms, shrub roses include any species of wild rose and old-fashioned varieties of bushy roses that pre-date large-flowered and cluster-flowered varieties. Modern shrub roses, retaining many of the characteristics of the old-fashioned types, are pruned in the same way. They generally make much bigger bushes than large-flowered and cluster-flowered types, and they do not require such regular or intensive pruning. You can also use this technique to prune larger English roses. The main objective of pruning a shrub rose is to prevent it from becoming too large or congested.

1 Most species and early shrub roses will continue to flower well, even without pruning, but they become large and congested. Pruning will improve the overall appearance and help to keep the shrub compact. After some years there will be a lot of very old wood and probably congested stems.

2 On an old plant cut out one or two of the oldest or most congested shoots, taking them back to the base. Cut out any dead or diseased wood at the same time. The rose shown here naturally produces a lot of cane-like stems from the base; others will have fewer but thicker stems, more like those on a large-flowered rose.

3 Shorten the main shoots by between a quarter and a half. If the shoot is 1.2m/4ft tall, cut off 30–60cm/1–2ft. If the shrub has produced a lot of side shoots, shorten these by about two-thirds. Side shoots about 30cm/12in long should be cut back to about 10cm/4in.

4 Even when pruning has been done, you may be left with a substantial framework of stems. This is normal because a shrub rose usually makes a large bush. With those that shoot freely from the base, you can be more drastic.

5 Annual pruning will ensure that there is plenty of vigorous, young growth from the base of the plant. It encourages the production of plenty of flowers, even close to the ground.

Pruning large-flowered (hybrid tea) roses

Large-flowered (hybrid tea) roses usually have large, fully double flowers with a high pointed centre, although as new varieties are developed the distinction between these and some cluster-flowered (floribunda) roses is becoming less clear than it used to be. A good rose catalogue will tell you whether your rose is a large-flowered variety, but it is not serious if you get it wrong and prune it as a cluster-flowered variety. There will still be a pleasing display of flowers in the summer.

Modern roses should be pruned fairly severely to enourage plenty of flowers on the new season's growth.

1 Large-flowered roses look very different depending on whether they have been regularly pruned. This rose has been pruned annually and is not particularly congested. A neglected rose will have more dead wood and crossing shoots to be removed. Otherwise, pruning is just the same. Start by cutting out dead or diseased shoots. This will make it easier to see what remains to be done.

2 Remove badly placed, crossing or very congested shoots. Most can be cut back to their point of origin, but if growth is sparse, cut to just above a healthy bud, close to the base. Prune out or shorten any very thin, spindly shoots. If there are plenty of other shoots, cut back to the point of origin. If there are few shoots, you may prefer to cut back to about two or three buds from the base of the shoot.

3 Prune all the main stems by about half or to within 20–25cm/8–10in of the ground. The exact amount you cut is not critical and is a matter of personal choice or trial and error. Wherever possible, prune to an outward-pointing bud to give the bush more spread rather than a congested centre.

4 The rose will look something like this after pruning. Although it is sparse at this stage, vigorous new growth will soon transform its appearance.

5 A few months later, if it has been pruned correctly, you can expect your large-flowered rose to look something like this. There is plenty of even, healthy growth springing from a balanced framework, and a good display of flowers.

Pruning cluster-flowered (floribunda) roses

Cluster-flowered (floribunda) roses have many flowers open at once in the same cluster, and they are noted for their prolific blooming. Although most varieties have flattish flowers with relatively few petals, some have flowers that look more like those of a large-flowered (hybrid tea) rose. If in doubt, a good rose catalogue will help you identify the rose in question.

Aim for a balanced framework when pruning, particularly for roses which can be seen from all sides.

A well-pruned cluster-flowered rose will produce plenty of healthy growth and an abundance of flowers.

1 Cluster-flowered roses often look more 'twiggy' than large-flowered varieties, regardless of how they were pruned the previous year. Do not be deterred if they appear to have a confusing tangle of thorny shoots. After removing unhealthy shoots, just start pruning from one side and work across each plant.

2 Start by cutting out dead or diseased shoots. Ignore dieback at the tips of shoots at this stage; they will probably be removed with the rest of the stem later. Cut these unwanted shoots back to their point of origin if there are plenty of other stems. Otherwise, cut to a point just above a healthy bud close to the base.

3 Remove any crossing or badly placed branches. Cut out completely if necessary or back to a bud point in a better direction. Remove any thin, spindly shoots coming from near the base of the bush.

4 Cut out all main stems back to about 45cm/18in, but use some discretion to reflect the size and vigour of the variety.

5 There will probably be some long side shoots remaining on the main stem. Shorten these by cutting off between one-third and two-thirds of their length. Cut back to an outward-facing bud.

6 The bushes will probably look like this after pruning. The framework is already well established, and the new growth will quickly restore the plants to their summer height.

Pruning climbing roses

Climbing roses can seem daunting to prune. Not only is there physically a lot of growth to deal with; there are also different techniques to use depending on the flowering habit of the variety. The first thing to decide is whether the rose is a once-flowering or repeat-flowering climber. Then follow the appropriate technique described here. You should find pruning fairly straightforward once you get started.

Repeat-flowering climbers

These generally bloom from mid-summer through to autumn, although after the first flush the flowers may be fewer and more sporadic. The terms perpetual flowering or remontant may also be used to describe these roses. They flower on new wood, but as relatively few new main shoots are produced, little pruning is required.

PRUNING REPEAT-FLOWERING CLIMBERS

1 During the summer, if you can, deadhead the rose as the flowers fade, cutting back to the nearest leaf. In early spring just shorten the shoots that flowered the previous summer if the plant is growing too tall. Drastic pruning or reshaping should not be necessary unless the rose has been neglected.

2 After shortening the tips of the main shoots, go along each stem and cut back those side shoots that flowered in summer to two or three buds. Remove dead or diseased wood and any badly positioned shoots. The basic outline may remain unchanged, but pruning ensures a good display of flowers in future years.

Once-flowering climbers

Climbing roses which flower only once in a year have a permanent framework of woody stems, usually with very few new shoots growing from the base. They need only minimal pruning for the first few years. Once-flowering climbers are best pruned in summer, once the flowering has finished for the year.

PRUNING ONCE-FLOWERING CLIMBERS

1 Because these climbers have a stable framework of woody shoots and are pruned in full leaf after flowering, they can often be intimidating to prune. Fortunately, they usually flower well with minimal pruning provided the plant is kept free of dead and diseased wood.

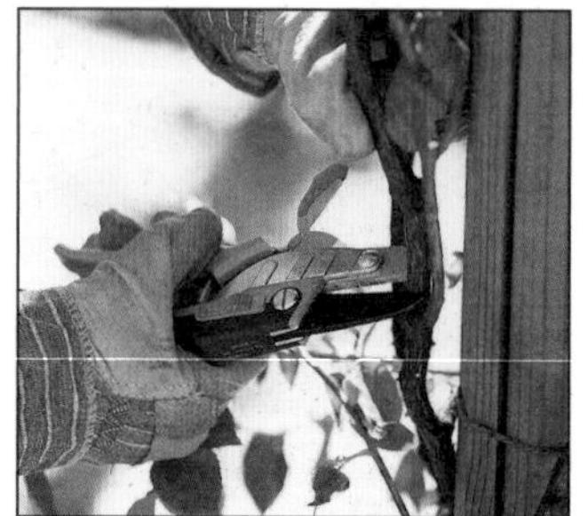

2 Try to cut out one or two of the oldest stems to increase the amount of new growth. If you can find a young replacement shoot near the base, cut to just above this. If there are no low-growing new shoots, choose a replacement perhaps 30–60cm/1–2ft up the stem.

3 Tie in the new growth to replace the shoot you have just removed. Do not remove more than one-third of the stems, otherwise flowering will suffer the next year. Go along the remaining stems and shorten the side shoots to leave two or three buds.

Pruning standard roses

Standard roses

The pruning of standard roses can appear confusing, and even gardeners who are confident about pruning bush roses sometimes feel uneasy about this task. However, do not be deterred by the apparent tangle of shoots. If you work methodically through the pruning there are few difficulties. Simply bear in mind that you are trying to form an attractive, rounded head.

Standard roses should be pruned in the late winter or early spring.

Pruning a weeping standard

Weeping standards are really rambling roses grafted on to a single stem. Like all rambling roses, they flower on shoots produced the previous year. For this reason weeping standards are pruned in summer or early autumn, when flowering has finished. They are not pruned when dormant, as other roses, including standard roses, are.

It is difficult to predict the vigour of the replacement shoots after pruning. If the growth seems uneven by spring, cut back the longest shoots to create a more balanced effect.

For both standard roses and weeping standards, pruning should be carried out annually, before the stems become congested and tangled and the head top-heavy.

Pruning is the ideal opportunity to examine the general health of the plant, looking for the first signs of any pests or diseases. Check, also, that the stake is sound and the ties are not too tight. Look for, and remove, any suckers arising from the main stem of the standard.

PRUNING A STANDARD ROSE

1 Shorten the main stems in the head to about six buds. Do not prune too hard as this may stimulate over-vigorous shoots that could spoil the shape.

2 Old plants may have areas of dead or diseased wood. Cut affected shoots back to healthy, outward-facing buds to encourage a good shape.

3 Shorten side shoots growing from the main stem to a couple of buds to stop growth becoming too congested.

Propagation

Propagating roses is extremely satisfying and it allows you to enjoy roses on a completely different level. Even if the new plants are not needed for your own garden, they make ideal gifts for friends.

Commercially, roses are propagated by grafting material from named varieties on to vigorous seedling rootstocks. This method is called budding. Rootstocks are not widely available outside the trade, although it may be possible to order them from some garden centres. Amateur gardeners usually choose to take hardwood or semi-ripe cuttings, or use the technique of layering.

When taking cuttings it is vital that you choose shoots that are free from diseases and pests and not too long between leaf joints (nodes). It's often best to take a cutting from the top of the plant, where it receives lots of light. Do not use any suckers that arise from the base of the plant: if the rose was grafted on to a different rootstock you may find you have propagated another plant entirely.

In general, only the most vigorous rose varieties will root readily and make good plants. But the only way to know for sure is to experiment, and propagation is often a matter of trial and error.

TAKING HARDWOOD CUTTINGS

1 Prepare a trench 23–30cm/9–12in deep in the open ground and line it to one-third of its depth with sharp sand.

2 Cut well-ripened, pencil-thick stems from the rose, remove the soft tip and trim to a length of about 23cm/9in, with the base of the cut just below a leaf joint. Remove any leaves that remain on the stem.

3 Dip the base of the cutting in hormone rooting powder. Tap off any excess powder.

4 Insert the cutting in the trench, leaving about 7.5cm/3in above the soil surface. Firm in and water well.

Hardwood cuttings

Hardwood cuttings are taken in autumn, at the end of the growing season, when top growth has ceased and fully ripened. They can be rooted in the open ground as long as there is some protection from strong winds.

Check the cuttings periodically during the winter. If a hard frost causes the soil to erode and crack open, it may be necessary to re-firm the cuttings. In very cold areas, protect the cuttings with a cloche.

The cuttings should be rooted by the following autumn, when they can be transferred to their final position in the garden if they are sufficiently developed. Alternatively, they can be allowed to grow on for another year.

Many gardeners find hardwood cuttings the best method of propagation as the aftercare required is minimal.

LAYERING

1 Select a pliable shoot that can be brought down to ground level from near the base of the plant. Cut off all the leaves and side shoots from a section about 30cm/1ft long.

2 Around the point where the stem will touch the ground, work in peat or an alternative to make the soil more friable.

3 With a sharp knife, cut a tongue in the wood on the underside of the stem.

4 Keep the tongue open with a small piece of wood – a matchstick, for example – and dust the cut surfaces with hormone rooting powder.

5 Bring the stem down to the ground. To keep the wound just below soil level, fasten down the stem with a length of wire bent into a U shape.

6 Bend the shoot tip upwards and secure it to a cane inserted in the ground with lengths of wire or horticultural string tied in figures of eight.

Layering

A good method for roses that have long, flexible stems that can be brought down to ground level. Climbing roses are obvious candidates for layering, and ground-cover roses – descendants of the climbing species – can also be increased by this technique. You may even find that some roses layer themselves in favourable conditions.

Layering is a simple technique, and it can be a more reliable one than taking cuttings because the new plant remains attached to the parent while rooting. It is, however, usually feasible to produce only a few new rose plants by this method because only a small number of stems is likely to be suitable.

Roses are best layered in late summer. The layers should have rooted by the following spring, when they can be severed from the parent, and potted up or grown on in a nursery bed until large enough to be planted out in their final position. Some rose growers find it most convenient to layer directly into a pot of compost. The container is buried in the ground, and the plant is layered as usual. Once the rose has rooted, it can be severed from the parent plant, and the whole pot is then dug up.

SEMI-RIPE CUTTINGS

1 Select a side shoot that is still green but beginning to turn woody at the base. Cut just above an outward-facing bud.

2 Trim the cutting at the base, just below a leaf joint.

3 Trim back the soft tip to leave a length of stem about 10cm/4in long.

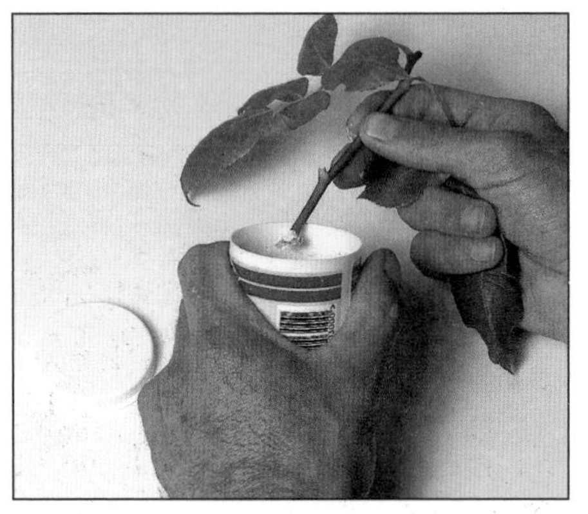

4 Remove the lower leaves and all the thorns, if any. Dip the base of the cutting in hormone rooting powder and tap off the excess.

5 Using a dibber, insert the cuttings up to two-thirds of their length in the rooting medium.

6 Firm the cuttings with your fingers, then spray them with a solution of copper fungicide, which will both moisten the soil mix and kill off any fungal spores and bacteria.

Semi-ripe cuttings

In very cold areas you may have more success propagating roses using the method of semi-ripe cuttings. The cuttings from this technique need more attention, both while rooting and when overwintering. Given proper care, however, a higher proportion of plants are likely to root by this method than by taking hardwood cuttings.

7 Label the cuttings, then tent the pot with a plastic bag to prevent moisture loss. Support the bag with sticks or wire hoops to prevent contact between the plastic and the leaves, because moisture will accumulate at that point and attract bacteria. Keep the cuttings in a shady, frost-free place until rooted.

■ BELOW
Roses such as this Portland rose 'Madame Knorr' are easy to propagate by taking semi-ripe cuttings.

■ ABOVE
After six to eight weeks the base of the cutting will callus over and new roots will begin to emerge.

Semi-ripe cuttings are taken from mid- to late summer as the current year's growth is beginning to ripen and become woody at the base but is still green and pliable. Root the cuttings in pots containing an inert mixture of peat and sharp sand. You need to check the cuttings periodically. Remove any fallen leaves that may rot and make sure the rooting medium stays fairly moist. Always water with a fungicidal solution to prevent disease.

Once the cuttings have rooted, usually by the following spring, they can be planted out and grown on in nursery beds, or potted up individually, using loam-based compost (soil mix).

Budding

Budding is a nurseryman's technique, widely practised within the trade as it allows saleable plants to be produced very quickly. Most amateur gardens prefer to take cuttings, which is a simpler but slower method of propagation. If you wish to increase your stock by budding you will need to acquire rootstocks, which are unfortunately not usually available to the public. The simplest method of accomplishing this is to contact a local commercial rose grower and ask if you can buy a rootstock. Patient gardeners can also raise their own stocks from seed.

Most roses are highly bred plants and have lost some of their vigour in the selection process. Budding is a technique that involves grafting buds from the parent plant (the scion) on to strongly growing rootstocks, usually of species roses such as *R. multiflora* or *R. canina*.

Budding is usually carried out from mid-summer onwards while the plants are still growing. You are more likely to be successful if you choose a wet day, when there is less chance of the propagating material drying out.

Select strong, healthy, well-ripened, non-flowering stems from the parent plant. To test for ripeness, bend one of the thorns. If the stem is ripe, the thorn will snap off cleanly. If the thorn is soft and flexible, the stem is not yet ripe enough.

The knife you use should be sharp and clean. Ragged cuts will not heal properly and could provide an entry point for disease.

If the union between the plants is a success, new growth will begin from the scion the following spring. Leave to develop *in situ* for at least a year before transferring to its final position.

PROPAGATION BY BUDDING

1 Cut a strong, ripe, healthy stem from the parent plant.

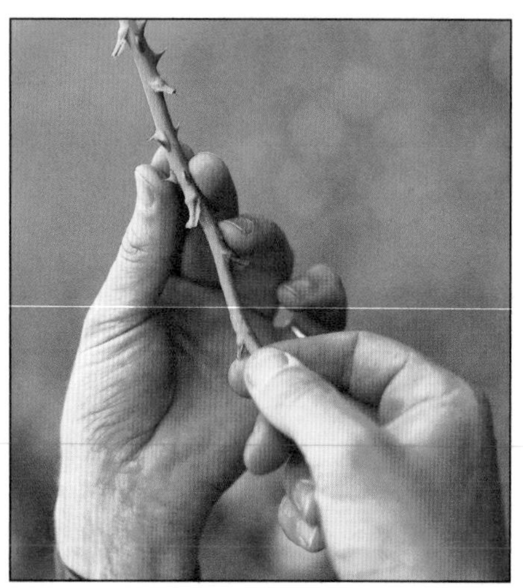

2 Trim off the leaves and snap off the thorns cleanly.

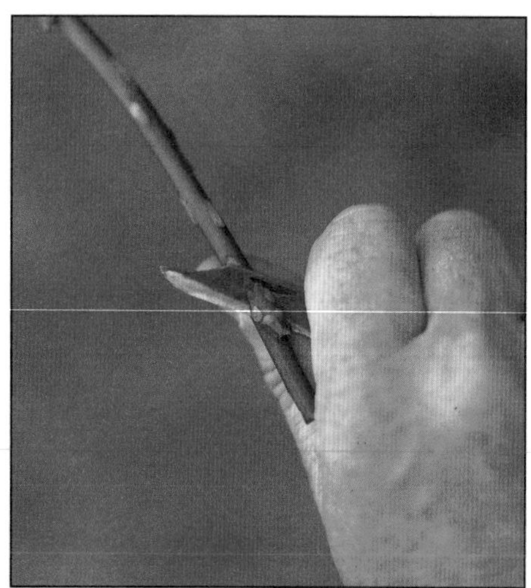

3 Hold the stem so that the growing point is facing towards you. Place the blade of a knife behind a dormant bud. Carefully draw the knife towards you to cut beneath the bud. Pull the knife to tear off a tail of bark.

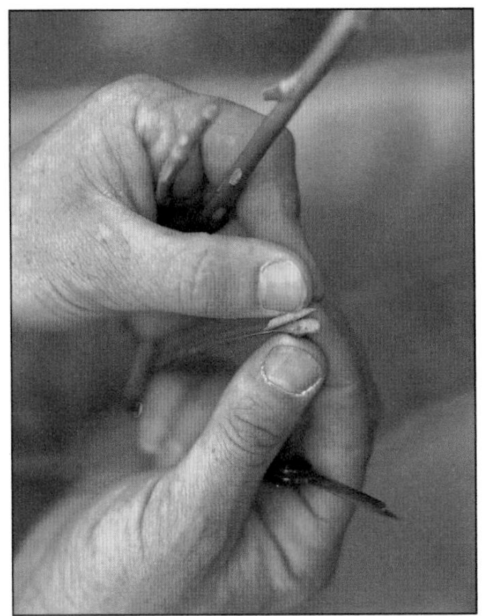

4 Pull off the pith behind the bud, using the knife if necessary.

5 Make a T-shaped cut in the rootstock, cutting no deeper than the bark. Ease back the bark with the tip of the knife.

6 Insert the bud into the cut on rootstock, the tail on top.

7 Trim back the tail so that it is level with the top of the T.

8 Bind the stem with a rubber tie and secure it with a pin. The rubber will stretch as the bud begins to swell and grow.

9 When the bud begins to grow strongly the following spring, remove the tie. Cut back the top growth of the rootstock and leave the rose as it is for about a year.

CREATING A NEW HYBRID ROSE

Hybridization

The process by which new plant varieties are produced is called hybridization. It can occur in the wild, where two compatible species grow in close proximity, but the vast majority of garden hybrids arise as a result of deliberate crossing.

Hybridization is a sexual method of producing new plants. In common with the majority of flowering plants, roses have flowers with both male and female reproductive parts. To produce fertile seeds, pollen, borne on the stamens (male) from one flower, is brought into contact with the stigmas (female) of another. Seed develops in the ovary below the stigmas. Seedlings will share some characteristics with both parents, without being identical to either.

Rose breeders practise hybridization extensively. In any one year hundreds of crosses are made, but only a few of the resulting plants have commercial potential. To be commercially viable a new rose must be vigorous, hardy and disease-resistant, and have good colour and scent. It must also be of sufficient novelty to distinguish it from existing roses. One or more of these attributes may be absent if the rose scores highly in other categories. All new roses have to undergo extensive trials before large-scale production can be considered. Given the fierce competition, it is unlikely that the amateur will raise a new rose with any significant future, but you can still produce good garden plants.

Since the rose as a genus has a vast gene pool and extensive interbreeding has already occurred, you can never be certain which characteristics will arise from any cross. Seedlings may bear no visible resemblance to either of their parents. The pedigrees of many modern roses are given in *Modern Roses*, published by the American Rose Society, but beyond a certain point, the ancestry of all rose hybrids is a matter if conjecture.

Theoretically, all roses should cross with each other, but some varieties are so highly bred that they are sterile (mules) or partly so. Also, some varieties make better pollen parents than seed parents and vice

1 Select the seed parent. Choose a flower that is not fully open and is unlikely to have been pollinated. Working from the outside, carefully pull off the petals.

2 Carefully remove the stamens with sterilized tweezers.

6 When it is fully open, pull all the petals to expose the reproductive parts.

7 Uncover the seed parent and brush the anthers of the pollen parent across the stigmas of the seed parent to transfer the pollen. Replace the bag and allow the hip to develop. Label the stem with the names of both parents.

3 When you have removed the stamens you should be left with the bare exposed stigmas.

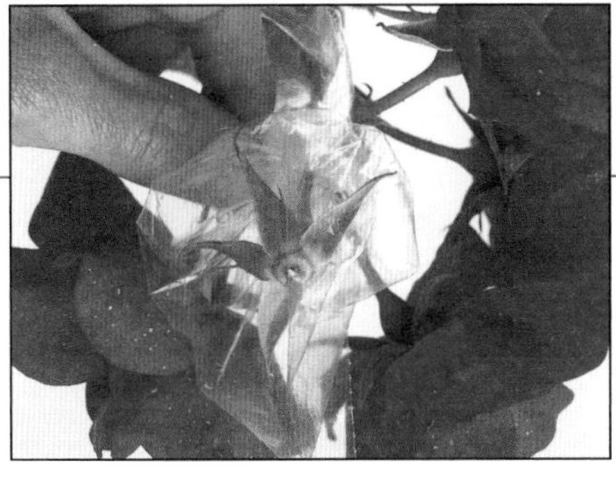

4 To prevent pollination from another source, cover the flower with a paper or plastic bag, secured with a wire tie.

5 Cut a flower that is not fully open from the pollen parent and keep it in water indoors.

8 Once the hip is ripe, cut it from the plant and slice it open to extract the seed. Mix the extracted seed with peat or an equivalent and grit or perlite in a plastic bag. Place it in the refrigerator for three or four weeks.

9 Sow the seed in trays or pots of seed compost and cover with grit.

10 Label the pots and place them in a cold frame to overwinter.

versa. In any breeding programme it is worth making the cross in both directions. When recording crosses, the convention is to cite the seed parent first. Thus, for example, label the seedlings 'Blue Moon' × 'Allgood' or 'Allgood' × 'Blue Moon'.

Rose seedlings can flower in their first year, although the blooms may not be typical. It will be a few years before you know whether you have produced an outstanding newcomer.

GENETIC ENGINEERING

Genetic engineering is a controversial technique by which specific genes (often from a different genus) are introduced into cells to ensure that a particular characteristic is inherited. Hitherto, its use has been largely confined to commercial, edible crop production, usually to promote disease resistance or a long shelf-life in foods.

There is every reason to suppose that in time, the techniques will be applied to ornamental plants, creating roses that, for instance, are particularly disease-resistant or hold their petals for a longer period. It should also be possible to extend the colour range to include the elusive blue. Genetic engineering requires laboratory conditions and is beyond the reach of the amateur gardener.

Care and maintenance

Apart from pruning, roses require little in the way of annual maintenance, but a little effort can improve the appearance of the rose garden and ensure that the plants remain in tiptop condition.

Weeding

It is essential to keep your roses weed-free, especially during the growing season. Repeated hoeing is not, however, the best way to do this because it is likely to damage the fine feeder roots that are close to the soil's surface. If you have a large area to look after, hoe if necessary, but avoid an area about 0.6–1m/2–3ft across around the base of each plant. This can then be weeded by hand. Weeds are easily pulled from the loose surface mulch.

Mulching

One of the most important requirements is to maintain a 5–7.5cm/2–3in mulch of well-rotted organic matter such as farmyard manure or garden compost at the root zone. An organic mulch helps to improve aeration and drainage, and retains moisture and nutrients. Temperature fluctuations at the root zone are reduced, keeping roots cool in summer and preventing them from freezing in winter. Finally, a mulch helps to keep down weeds. Non-organic mulches can also be used to improve the appearance of the bed.

Chipped bark is a popular and efficient mulch, and it looks attractive. Cocoa shells can also be used, but may blow about when dry. Plastic mulching sheets are effective but are visually unappealing. They are best covered with a decorative layer of chipped bark.

Mulches should be applied each or every other year around the base of the plant, in early spring when the weather is fine. The soil should be moist but not waterlogged or frozen. If you apply a mulch to dry soil it will reduce the amount of natural rainfall that reaches the roots.

Watering

Roses need adequate moisture throughout the growing season. Plants in open ground, especially if well mulched, seldom need additional water except during their first season or when hot, dry weather is prolonged. In these circumstances, the soil may be dry to some depth, so applications of water must be copious enough to penetrate the soil around the root zone. Watering too little causes the plant's roots to grow up towards the surface in search of moisture, thus becoming vulnerable to the damaging effects of heat and drought. As a guide, apply 4–5 litres/1 gallon for a rose bush, three times this amount for a climber.

If water has to be rationed, always give priority to roses planted within the last year. More established bushes, which have deep roots, are better able to cope with dry soil.

Plants in containers rely heavily on the gardener to be conscientious in watering. They have only a small volume of soil to exploit for moisture, and the soil in pots dries rapidly in

■ LEFT
Remove weeds by hand so that you do not damage fine feeder roots.

warm, dry weather. This is especially true of roses grown in hanging baskets. Terracotta pots, which are permeable to water, need more attention than plastic ones. During the summer all container-grown roses should be checked and watered thoroughly, every day if necessary.

Feeding

Roses are 'hungry' shrubs and require feeding if they are to grow to their maximum potential. If any of the important nutrients are deficient the plant will have weak or stunted growth, small or discoloured leaves and small, poor-quality flowers.

■ ABOVE
Apply fertilizer to the base of the plant and 'tickle' it in with a hand fork.

Feeding starts at planting time. Plenty of humus-forming material, such as well-rotted manure or garden compost, will add nutrients as well as improving the structure of the soil. The initial nutrients are soon depleted, but a soil with a high organic content is more likely to retain nutrients that you apply later. It is possible to grow good roses simply by applying plenty of garden compost each year, but for optimum performance, use a rose fertilizer. Apply the first dose in spring before the leaves are fully open, and another in early or mid-summer when the roses are blooming freely. Always follow the instructions on the packet.

Avoid feeding in late summer as this may encourage the plant to produce soft growth that could be damaged in a cold winter. However, if your roses are really not growing and flowering well, an application of a high-potash fertilizer in late summer or early autumn will help late-formed shoots to ripen before the onset of winter.

Liquid feeding will give roses a useful quick-acting boost, so if other garden plants are being fed from a hose-end dilutor, for example, give the roses another dose if they do not appear to be in tiptop condition.

■ ABOVE
Cut back faded flowers to a bud in the axil of the nearest full-sized leaf.

Soil nutrients in containers tend to leach away more quickly than in the open ground, so in addition to routine applications of fertilizer, every two or three weeks during the growing season you should give the container rose a liquid feed.

Deadheading

It is particularly important for roses that flower repeatedly to be deadheaded. If they are allowed to produce hips, the energy expended in seed production is unavailable for further production of flowers.

For cluster-flowered roses, removing the central flower of the cluster as it fades will improve the appearance of the group. When the entire cluster has faded, remove the whole head, cutting back to a healthy bud or full-sized leaf. After the main flush of flowers, feed the roses well.

Pests, diseases and other disorders

Most roses are prone to a number of pests and diseases, but fortunately, most of these are easy to control. The incidence of disease and pest attack depends to some extent on climatic and regional variations – blackspot, for example, is more prevalent in some parts of the country than in others; mildew is more likely to be a problem if the weather is dry; and the aphid population will be affected by the winter survival of their predators.

As soon as the weather warms up, watch for signs of pest and disease infestation. Treat immediately, before population numbers have time to build up. Aphids can be particularly damaging, as they attack young shoot tips and cause subsequent distortion of growth.

In some seasons poor weather provides perfect conditions for the spread of fungal diseases, especially blackspot. An annual tar-oil winter wash applied to the stems and surrounding soil will reduce the reservoir of fungal spores and the need for extensive spraying with fungicide later on.

Some rose varieties are more susceptible to problems than others, but well-fed roses that are growing strongly can usually survive any attack, provided you act quickly. In addition, modern roses have a greatly improved disease-resistance.

Maintaining good standards of garden hygiene decreases the likelihood and the severity of any problems. Regularly clear up all plant debris, such as fallen leaves, both from the roses and also from other plants, as these may rot and harbour disease. You should also burn or otherwise dispose of any rose prunings for the same reason – do not put them on the compost heap. Make sure that the plants have enough space around them to ensure good air circulation. You may need to rethink your planting scheme if they become overcrowded as they develop.

Systemic insecticides and fungicides are applied as a spray and are absorbed by the plant. They do not kill the pest or disease directly, so their effect is not immediate. Repeated applications are usually necessary. Always follow the manufacturer's instructions.

The following are some of the problems which you are most likely to encounter. Most can be easily remedied if caught early.

■ RIGHT
Pre-empt problems by spraying against aphids in spring.

Aphids

The aphid that is most likely to attack roses is the greenfly, and these sap-sucking insects are usually spotted near the start of the season, clustering at the ends of stems and developing flower buds. They cause stunting and distortion of growth and may transmit viruses.

The aphids seen early in the year usually result from a failure to destroy prunings from the previous season that may harbour eggs. In practice, however, aphids are virtually endemic, and you are likely to encounter aphids every season.

To control aphids spray plants with a proprietary systemic insecticide as soon as you notice an infestation, and repeat as directed by the manufacturer. A specific aphicide containing pirimicarb will leave beneficial insects such as ladybirds and lacewings unharmed.

■ BELOW
Neatly notched leaves indicate the activities of leaf-cutting bees.

Organic gardeners may remove aphids by hand, spray with soft soap or use an insecticide based on derris or pyrethrum. Sometimes spraying with plain water will disperse the pest, but such treatment will have to be repeated daily. Although infestations may be severe, the pest is easy to control, and long-term damage can easily be avoided.

Leaf-cutting bee

Neat, semicircular or circular holes are cut out from the leaf margins. The bees use the portions of leaf to make nests for their young. The damage is largely cosmetic and will not affect the health of established plants. If the damage is severe, disturb the insects with a fly swat, taking care not to be stung. Bees are beneficial pollinators and do not justify the use of chemicals.

Leaf-rolling sawfly

In late spring or early summer rose leaflets become tightly rolled around freshly laid eggs. The caterpillar eats the leaves as it emerges.

At the leaf-rolling stages, leaves can be picked off if the infestation is light. For more severe attacks, leave the foliage in place and spray with a systemic insecticide. You will not reverse damage already caused, but you will reduce the emerging population that lays eggs in subsequent years. If you have had the problem one year, you can expect it the next, although you can achieve some protection by spraying the undersides of the leaves with insecticide in late spring or very early summer before the adults lay eggs.

Balling

Flowers have a slack appearance, and the petals turn brown and cling together so that the flowers fail to open properly. This may happen if there is prolonged wet weather while the buds are developing or if rain is followed by hot sun. Aphid infestation early in the season can also lead to balling. Some roses are more susceptible than others.

This disorder is impossible to control. Balling is a seasonal problem, which does not affect the overall health of the plant, but you should remove balled flowers that may otherwise rot and allow diseases to take hold. Balled flowers are sometimes infected with fungi and dieback may occur.

Roses with very delicate petals are the most susceptible to balling, but positioning them where they will receive adequate sunlight and ventilation to dry the blooms will help to minimize the risk of rain damage. Deadhead promptly, by cutting back to a healthy bud or leaf.

■ LEFT
Balling is caused by wet weather. It is not a common problem, but some rose varieties are prone to it.

Blackspot

From the middle of summer onwards black spots or patches develop on the leaves of affected plants and sometimes on the stems. The leaves turn yellow and eventually drop off. Plants left untreated will die back.

Blackspot is caused by a fungus that overwinters in the soil and enters the plant during the growing season. Leaving infected prunings on the ground increases the likelihood of its occurrence.

Remove all infected leaves and stems and destroy them. Spray the plant with a fungicide after spring pruning, and repeat according to the manufacturer's instructions. Rake up and burn all fallen leaves in autumn, and apply a tar-oil winter wash. If you need to cut the plant hard back to remove affected stems, feed and water it well to encourage recovery. Blackspot is more common in certain geographical areas, and some rose varieties are more susceptible than others. In severe cases, replace with the rose with disease-resistant and guaranteed disease-free stock.

■ RIGHT

The early stages of blackspot. Preventative measures and good hygiene help to reduce the incidence of the disease.

Dieback

Flower buds, if present, do not mature but wither. Beginning at the tip of the stem, leaves begin to wither and drop off. The stem itself droops and may blacken. If left untreated, rose diseases such as blackspot and mildew can lead to dieback, but the condition may also be due to other fungi or bacteria, which gain entry through pruning wounds, frost damage or a lack of nutrients, particularly potassium and phosphorus, in the soil.

Cut back all affected growth to clean, healthy wood – the pith will be white, with no sign of brown staining – then feed the plant well. If dieback occurs in autumn, do not feed until the following spring because any new growth you promote will itself be susceptible to winter frost damage.

Powdery mildew

Affected roses have a whitish-grey powdery fungal growth on the upper surfaces of leaves and on both surfaces of young leaves. Affected leaves may drop prematurely. It may also affect stems and flower buds, and if it is left untreated, the mildew could cover the entire plant. The damage is most likely to be caused by various fungi that thrive in dry soil, where the air is warm, dry and stagnant. It occurs from early summer onwards. Some rambling roses are prone to mildew after flowering, when they produce a mass of vigorous new shoots that can become congested. The problem is likely to be worse when they are grown against walls and air circulation is poor and the soil is dry at the foot of the wall, but it can be lessened by appropriate pruning.

Control by spraying with a proprietary fungicide. Thin out congested growth. Where the overall planting is thick and air circulation is therefore poor, replant to ensure that there is more space around the plants. Mulch well to conserve soil moisture and water thoroughly in prolonged dry periods and avoid using high-nitrogen fertilizers.

■ BELOW
Rust appears as orange spots on leaf stalks and surfaces in early summer.

Proliferation

In this unusual condition the stem continues to grow through the open flower, producing another bud or cluster of buds. This may be caused if the stem is damaged while it is growing, either by frost or a virus.

Cut off the affected stems. If only a few stems are affected, further steps are unnecessary, but if the whole plant has the condition, it is likely that the culprit is a virus, and the only remedy is to dig up the entire plant and destroy it.

Rust

Orange spots that turn to black appear on leaf stalks and leaf surfaces in early summer, with orange pustules on the undersides of the leaves. Leaves may drop prematurely.

Spores are spread by wind and rain and need damp, humid conditions to thrive. Do not plant roses too closely together and keep bushes open-centred for good air circulation. Prune out infected stems in spring and burn prunings promptly. Spray with a suitable fungicide.

Soil sickness

Rose soil sickness is sometimes also referred to as rose replant disease. Roses sometimes suddenly fail to thrive and begin to die back. The causes are complex but are thought to be a combination of soil nutrient exhaustion, a build up of soil-borne nematodes (eelworms), viruses and fungi. These micro-organisms become particularly virulent when in contact with the newly formed feeder roots of a freshly planted young rose. It usually occurs in ground on which roses have been grown for a number of years.

There is no cure, so the problem should be avoided in the first place. Plant new roses in soil that has not been used to grow roses for at least seven years. Alternatively, dig up and discard the affected roses, replace the top 60cm/24in of soil and replant with a different type of rose.

■ LEFT
Proliferation, an unusual physiological disorder, occurs when a stem continues to grow through an existing flower.

Suckering

Strong shoots may arise from the rootstock, often at some distance from the plant. They also occur on the main stems of standards. Left in place, they will rob the rose of nutrients. Suckers arise when the roots are damaged, usually through digging around the plant. Modern rootstocks have a lesser tendency to sucker, but suckers are always likely to occur on standards, since the rootstock is above ground level.

Scrape away the soil around the sucker until you find its point of origin. Pull it sharply away from the roots. On standards, rub out emerging buds on the main stem or, if they are long shoots, cut them back to their point of origin.

Calendar

■ BELOW
A hedge of *Rosa rugosa* in late summer. The tomato-like hips redden as the season advances until, in autumn, they provide a display to match that of the summer flowers.

Early spring

Improve the soil and plant new stock. On established plants, cut out any dead, diseased or damaged wood and shorten the remaining stems (ideally before the new leaves emerge, but after any danger of frost has passed). Fork fertilizer around the base of the roses as growth emerges, water in well and apply a 5–7.5cm/2–3in layer of mulch at the base of established plants. Cut back the rootstock on roses that were budded during the previous summer and that are showing signs of fresh growth. Renovate any old or neglected plants by pruning and feeding. Plant container-grown roses in the garden and also any bare-root roses that have not already been planted. In areas with very cold winters, prune repeat-flowering roses.

Mid- to late spring

Continue to plant new container-grown stock, remembering to keep them well watered until they are established. Check for and begin to control aphid infestations, leaf-rolling sawfly and blackspot. Remove any suckers. Apply a preventative fungicide as leaves emerge.

Mid-summer

Deadhead regularly and boost with rose fertilizer after the first flush of flowers. If necessary, prune after flowering. Increase your stock by taking semi-ripe cuttings (vigorous types only) or by budding. Keep a watch for suckers. Plant new stocks (container-grown roses only). In periods of prolonged hot, dry weather, water roses in open ground. Water roses in containers regularly and feed with liquid fertilizer. Continue to check for and control aphids, blackspot, rust and mildew. Visit garden centres and other gardens, read new specialist catalogues and begin to plan for autumn ordering, especially of roses that may be less readily available in local garden centres.

Old roses
Deadhead repeat-flowering roses and any others not grown for their decorative hips. Trim hedges after flowering unless grown for their hips. Thin twiggy growth on gallicas to improve air circulation.

Climbing roses
Shear over large ramblers. Tie in new shoots of climbers throughout the growing season. Layer ground-cover roses after flowering.

■ BELOW
In summer, tie in the shoots of climbers while they are still young and flexible.

Late summer

Water plants regularly if the weather is hot. Continue to take semi-ripe cuttings of vigorous plants or layer them if suitable.

Old roses
Peg down stems of hybrid perpetuals and other types that produce long, flexible stems. Tie in strong, new shoots on roses trained as climbers.

Climbing roses
Tie in strong new shoots to extend the framework.

Early autumn

Fork in bonemeal around the base of the plants, water in well and mulch with garden compost. Apply a high-potash fertilizer to plants that are not growing well. Rake up and burn fallen rose leaves. Take hardwood cuttings of vigorous roses. Place orders with specialist nurseries.

Climbing roses
Prune to remove all the old, unproductive wood, cutting back to the base where necessary. Tie in shoots securely to prevent damage during winter gales.

Mid- to late autumn

In climates with a mild winter only, begin pruning repeat-flowering roses. Begin to dig over and improve soil ready for new plantings. Begin planting bare-root roses; the planting season extends to early spring during periods when the soil is not too wet, dry or frozen.

Mid-winter

Browse through mail order catalogues for any last-minute orders. Plant bare-root or container-grown roses in periods of good weather, when the soil is not waterlogged, dry or frozen. Apply a winter wash of tar oil if wished to reduce the need for fungicide sprays later in the season.

Late winter

In exposed sites, shorten the stems of specimen roses to prevent wind-rock. In frosty weather, if the soil surface freezes and cracks, firm in hardwood cuttings. In mild areas finish pruning repeat-flowering roses. Improve the soil for new spring plantings by incorporating organic material. Plant roses that were ordered earlier in the winter or, if necessary, heel them in until weather conditions improve.

Old roses
Tidy up hedges, such as *Rosa rugosa*, that have ornamental hips and were thus not pruned after flowering.

■ LEFT
Plant early-flowering and late-flowering rose varieties in the same bed to extend the season of colourful displays from early summer right through to late autumn.

Other Recommended Roses

In addition to the roses that are illustrated in the individual directory sections, the following roses are also recommended. Synonyms and the date of introduction, where known, follow the name of the rose in parentheses. The dimensions of the rose under good growing conditions are given at the end of the description. The first figure indicates the rose's ultimate height, the second its spread.

■ RIGHT
The large, vivid yellow flowers of 'Freedom' make this rose a good choice for brightening up a garden.

Other recommended old roses

'Andersonii'

'Bloomfield Abundance'

'Agnes' (1922) Rugosa. Large, scented, double, pale yellow, occasionally buff, flowers appear in summer. A thorny rose.
1.8 × 1.2m/6 × 4ft.

'Andersonii' (uncertain) *Canina* hybrid. Lightly scented, single, deep pink flowers appear in mid-summer, followed by red hips in autumn.
2.1 × 2.4m/7 × 8ft.

'Blanche Double de Coubert' (1892) Rugosa. Sweetly scented, semi-double, white flowers open flat from pointed, pinkish buds from summer to autumn.
1.5 × 1.2m/5 × 4ft.

'Bloomfield Abundance' (1920) Polyantha. Delicate, lightly scented, double, pale soft-pink flowers open from buds with long, feathery calyces from summer to autumn.
1.8 × 1.5m/6 × 5ft.

'Blush Damask' (uncertain) Damask. Sweetly scented, fully double, deep lilac-pink flowers are produced in mid-summer.
1.2 × 1.2m/4 × 4ft.

'Camaïeux' (1830) Gallica. Fragrant, fully double, white flowers, striped and splashed with crimson, are produced in mid-summer.
1.2 × 1m/4 × 3ft.

'Celsiana' (before 1750) Damask. Strongly fragrant, semi-double, deep rose-pink flowers are borne in clusters in mid-summer.
1.5 × 1.2m/5 × 4ft.

× ***centifolia*** (uncertain) Centifolia. Strongly scented, fully double, soft-pink flowers are produced in mid-summer.
1.5 × 1.5m/5 × 5ft.

× ***centifolia*** **'Muscosa'** (common moss rose, syn. 'Old Pink Moss'; around 1696). Moss. Fragrant, fully double, clear-pink flowers are borne in mid-summer.
1.5 × 1.5m/5 × 5ft.

'Commandant Beaurepaire' (syn. 'Panachée d'Angers'; 1874) Bourbon. Fragrant, double, deep pink flowers, splashed and striped with purple, maroon and paler pink, appear in mid-summer and, more sporadically, in autumn.
1.8 × 1.5m/6 × 5ft.

'Comtesse du Caÿla' (1902) China. Fragrant, semi-double, copper-orange flowers, which fade to salmon-pink, are produced from summer to autumn.
1.5 × 1.5m/5 × 5ft.

'Cornelia' (1925) Hybrid musk. Sweetly scented, double flowers, carried from summer to autumn, fade from apricot-pink to creamy pink.
1.5 × 1.5m/5 × 5ft.

'De Meaux' (pompon rose; syn. *R.* × *centifolia* var. *pomponia*, 'Rose de Meaux'; 1789) Centifolia. Sweetly scented, fully double, soft-pink flowers appear in mid-summer.
1 × 1m/3 × 3ft.

'De Rescht' (uncertain) Damask Portland. Heavily scented, fully double, deep magenta-red flowers appear in mid-summer then intermittently until autumn.
1 × 1m/3 × 3ft.

ecae Species. Small, scented, single, cupped, brilliant yellow flowers are borne in late spring to early summer. Delicate mid-green foliage with reddish stems. A tender plant, benefiting from shelter.
1.5 × 1.2m/5 × 4ft.

'Empereur du Maroc' (1858) Hybrid perpetual. Intensely fragrant, fully double, quartered-rosette flowers of a rich red, almost purple, colour appear in mid-summer and again in autumn.
1.2 × 1m/4 × 3ft.

'Felicia' (1928) Hybrid musk. Sweetly scented, fully double, pale pink flowers are carried from summer to autumn. Abundant foliage is greyish-green.
1.5 × 2.1m/5 × 7ft.

'Ferdinand Pichard' (1921) Bourbon. Richly scented, loosely double, deep pink flowers, striped

'Blanche Double de Coubert'

'Fru Dagmar Hastrup'

with crimson and purple, appear from mid-summer to autumn.
1.2 × 1.2m/4 × 4ft.

foetida (Austrian briar, Austrian yellow rose) Species. Unpleasantly scented, single, bright yellow flowers are borne in early summer. 'Persiana' is a popular cultivar.
1.5 × 1.5m/5 × 5ft.

× ***francofurtana*** (syn. 'Empress Josephine'; early 19th century) Gallica. Lightly scented, loosely double, bright pink flowers, veined with deeper pink, are produced in mid-summer.
1.2 × 1.2m/4 × 4ft.

'Frau Karl Druschki' (syn. 'Reine des Neiges', 'Snow Queen'; 1901) Hybrid perpetual. Scentless, fully double, pure-white flowers emerge from pink-tinged buds in summer.
1.2 × 1.2m/4 × 4ft.

'Fru Dagmar Hastrup' (syn. 'Frau Dagmar Hartopp'; 1914) Rugosa. Scented, single, light pink flowers are borne in summer and autumn.
1 × 1.2m/3 × 4ft.

'Frühlingsmorgen' (syn. 'Spring Morning'; 1942) Pimpinellifolia hybrid. Lightly scented, single, pale pink to creamy white flowers are carried in late spring. A thorny rose with greyish-green foliage
1.8 × 1.5m/6 × 5ft.

'Général Kléber' (1856) Centifolia moss. Large, fragrant, fully double, soft-pink flowers with a silky sheen are borne in mid-summer.
1.5 × 1.5m/5 × 5ft.

'Georg Arends' (1910) Hybrid perpetual. Fragrant, fully double, soft-pink flowers appear from mid- to late summer. Nearly thornless.
1.8 × 1.8m/6 × 6ft.

'Gloire de France' (syn. 'Fanny Bias'; before 1819) Gallica. Very fragrant, fully double, pale mauve-pink flowers appear in mid-summer.
1 × 1m/3 × 3ft.

'Great Maiden's Blush' (syn. 'Cuisse de Nymphe', 'La Séduisante'; 15th century or earlier) Alba. Sweetly fragrant, rosette, double, soft-pink flowers appear in mid-summer or later.
1.5 × 1.5m/5 × 5ft or more.

jacksonii **'Max Graf'** (syn. 'Max Graf'; 1919) Rugosa. Fragrant, single, deep pink flowers with golden stamens are produced throughout summer. 0.6 × 2.4m/2 × 8ft.

'Katharina Zeimet' (syn. 'White Baby Rambler') Polyantha. Sprays of many sweetly scented, small, double, cupped, white flowers are borne almost continuously from summer to autumn.
50 × 50cm/20 × 20in or more.

'Lady Hillingdon' (1910) Tea. Fragrant, semi-double, apricot-yellow flowers open from long, pointed, copper-orange buds from summer until autumn or later.
75 × 60cm/2½ × 2ft.

'Madame Knorr' (syn. 'Comte de Chambord'; 1860) Portland. Sweetly scented, fully double, deep pink flowers are produced in summer with a repeat flowering in autumn.
1.2 × 1.2m/4 × 4ft.

'Madame Pierre Oger' (1878) Bourbon. Sweetly scented, fully double, pale creamy pink flowers are produced from summer to autumn. Leaves are light green. A good pillar rose.
1.8 × 1.2m/6 × 4ft.

'Marchesa Boccella' (syn. 'Jacques Cartier'; 1866) Damask Portland. Strongly scented, fully double, clear-pink flowers, paler at the edges, are borne in summer and again, but unreliably, in autumn.
1.2 × 1.2m/4 × 4ft.

'Madame Knorr'

'Mevrouw Nathalie Nypels' (syn. 'Nathalie Nypels'; 1919) Polyantha. Sweetly scented, semi-double, clear-pink flowers, fading to blush pink, are borne from summer to autumn.
60 × 60cm/2 × 2ft.

'Mousseline' (syn. 'Alfred de Dalmas'; 1855) Portland moss. Fragrant, semi-double, cupped soft blush-pink to creamy white flowers are produced in mid-summer.
1.2 × 1.2m/4 × 4ft.

moyesii (1903) Species. Virtually scentless, single, crimson flowers with yellow stamens appear from early to mid-summer, followed in autumn by flagon-shaped, brilliant scarlet hips.
2.4 × 1.5m/8 × 5ft.

'Mrs John Laing' (1887) Hybrid perpetual. Large, sweetly scented, fully double, clear-pink flowers are freely produced from summer to autumn. Light green foliage.
1 × 1m/3 × 3ft.

odorata **'Viridiflora'** (green rose; syn. 'Viridiflora', *R. chinensis* 'Viridiflora', 'Lü E'; before 1833) China. Curious rather than beautiful, scentless, double, purple-tinged green "flowers" (in reality modified leaves) are produced from summer to autumn.
1 × 0.6m/3 × 2ft.

'Penelope' (1924) Hybrid musk. Large, sweetly scented, semi-double, pale creamy pink flowers are borne in clusters from summer to autumn.
1 × 1m/3 × 3ft.

'Petite de Hollande' (syn. 'Normandica', 'Petite Junon de Hollande', 'Pompon des Dames'; about 1800) Centifolia. Clusters of small, sweetly scented, double, pompon-like flowers, clear-pink with darker centres, are borne in summer.
1 × 1m/3 × 3ft.

pimpinellifolia **'Plena'** Species. Double, cupped, creamy white flowers are borne early in summer, followed by blackish hips. Rather a thorny rose, but with abundant small dark green leaves.
1 × 1.2m/3 × 4ft.

moyesii

'Pink Grootendorst' (1923) Rugosa. Scentless, carnation-like, double, clear-pink flowers have fimbriated (fringed) edges and are produced from summer to autumn.
1.8 × 1.5m/6 × 5ft.

primula (incense rose; 1911) Species. Lightly scented, single, pale yellow flowers appear in late spring. The leaves are aromatic when wet.
1.8 × 1.8m/6 × 6ft.

'Reine des Violettes' (syn. 'Queen of the Violets'; 1860) Hybrid perpetual. Heavily scented, fully double, deep red flowers, ageing to dove-grey, are produced from summer to autumn.
1.8 × 1.8m/6 × 6ft.

'Reine Victoria' (syn. 'La Reine Victoria'; 1872) Bourbon. Sweetly scented, fully double, pink flowers are produced from summer to autumn.
1.8 × 1.2m/6 × 4ft.

rubiginosa (sweet briar, eglantine; syn. *R. eglanteria*) Species. Clusters of lightly scented, single, pink flowers are carried amid fragrant leaves in mid-summer, followed by scarlet hips.
2.4 × 2.4m/8 × 8ft.

'Saint Nicholas' (1950) Damask. Fragrant, semi-double, rich pink flowers with yellow stamens appear in mid-summer, followed by red hips in the autumn. Leaves are dark green and plentiful.
1.2 × 1.2m/4 × 4ft.

'Sarah van Fleet' (1926) Rugosa. Sweetly scented, light pink flowers open to reveal yellow stamens from summer to autumn.
1.8 × 1.2m/6 × 4ft or more.

'Sneezy' (uncertain) Polyantha. Masses of single, pink flowers are produced from summer to autumn.
30 × 30cm/12 × 12in.

'Souvenir du Docteur Jamain' (1865) Hybrid perpetual. Fragrant, fully double, wine-red flowers are carried in summer and autumn.
1.8 × 1.8m/6 × 6ft.

'Spong' (1805) Centifolia. Small, rounded, pompon-like, clear-pink flowers are carried amongst abundant foliage in mid-summer.
1.2 × 1m/4 × 3ft.

'The Bishop' (uncertain) Centifolia. Fragrant, fully double, cerise-purple

odorata 'Viridiflora'

flowers appear in mid-summer and then fade to lilac-mauve.
1.5 × 1m/5 × 3ft.

'Tour de Malakoff' (1856) Centifolia. Heavily scented, fully double, cupped, rich magenta-purple flowers, which age to dove-grey, are produced in mid-summer.
1.8 × 1.5m/6 × 5ft.

'Variegata di Bologna' (1909) Bourbon. Heavily scented, fully double, pale lilac-pink flowers, striped with intense crimson-purple, appear in mid-summer and autumn. Prone to blackspot.
1.8 × 1.8m/6 × 6ft.

'Yvonne Rabier' (1910) Polyantha. Lightly scented, double, creamy white flowers are borne from summer to autumn. Foliage is bright green and plentiful.
45 × 40cm/18 × 16in.

Other recommended modern roses

'Abbeyfield Rose' (syn. 'Cochrose'; 1985) Large-flowered or hybrid tea. Lightly scented, fully double, deep pink flowers are borne from summer to autumn. Good for bedding. 75 × 60cm/2½ × 2ft.

'Allgold' (1956) Cluster-flowered or floribunda. Scented, double, bright yellow flowers are produced throughout summer and autumn. 75 × 50cm/30 × 20in.

'Anisley Dickson' (syn. 'Dickimono', 'Dicky', 'Müncher Kindl'; 1983) Cluster-flowered or floribunda. Only lightly scented, double, salmon-pink flowers are produced from summer to autumn. Good in containers. 1 × 0.75m/3 × 2½ft.

'Anna Livia' (syn. 'Kormetter', 'Trier 2000'; 1985) Cluster-flowered or floribunda. Sprays of scented, double, clear-pink flowers are carried from summer to autumn. Suitable for a low hedge. 75 × 60cm/2½ × 2ft.

'Anvil Sparks' (syn. 'Ambossfunken') Large-flowered or hybrid tea. Shapely buds open to coral-red flowers striped and spotted with yellow. Healthy. 1 × 1m/3 × 3ft.

'Bright Smile' (syn. 'Dicdance'; 1980) Cluster-flowered or floribunda. Fragrant, semi-double, clear bright yellow flowers, which are rain-resistant, open flat from summer to autumn. Good disease resistance. 45 × 45cm/18 × 18in.

'Carefree Beauty' (syn. 'Bucbi'; 1977) Shrub. Fragrant, semi-double, creamy buff-pink flowers are carried on spreading stems all summer. 1.2 × 1.2m/4 × 4ft.

'Champagne Cocktail' (syn. 'Horflash'; 1985) Cluster-flowered or floribunda. Fragrant, double, light yellow flowers, suffused with pink, appear from summer to autumn. Good for bedding. 1 × 0.6m/3 × 2ft.

'Chanelle' (1959) Cluster-flowered or floribunda. Fragrant, semi-double to double, creamy buff-pink flowers are borne through summer and autumn. Good disease resistance. 75 × 60cm/2½ × 2ft.

'City of Leeds' (1966) Cluster-flowered or floribunda. Lightly scented, semi-double, salmon-pink flowers are produced from summer to autumn. Good for bedding. 75 × 60cm/2½ × 2ft.

'City of London' (syn. 'Harukfore'; 1988) Cluster-flowered or floribunda. Sweetly scented, semi-double to double, soft-pink flowers appear from summer to autumn. A good bedding rose or grow as a specimen plant. 2.4 × 1.2m/8 × 4ft.

'Deep Secret'

'Congratulations' (syn. 'Korlift', 'Sylvia'; 1978) Large-flowered or hybrid tea. Fragrant, fully double, neat, deep pink flowers are borne from summer to autumn. 1.2 × 1m/4 × 3ft or more.

'Crimson Glory' (1935) Large-flowered or hybrid tea. Fragrant, fully double, deep red flowers, good for cutting, appear all summer. 60 × 60cm/2 × 2ft.

'Dawn Chorus' (syn. 'Dicquasar'; 1993) Large-flowered or hybrid tea. Only lightly scented, double, orange flowers, with yellow petal reverses, are borne from summer to autumn. 75 × 60cm/2½ × 2ft.

'Dearest' (1960) Cluster-flowered or floribunda. Fragrant, double, clear-pink flowers are produced from summer to autumn. 60 × 60cm/2 × 2ft.

'Deep Secret' (syn. 'Mildred Scheel'; 1977) Large-flowered or hybrid tea. Fragrant, double, deep red flowers are borne from summer to autumn. Good for cutting.
1 × 0.75m/3 × 2½ft.

'Disco Dancer' (syn. 'Dicinfra'; 1984) Cluster-flowered or floribunda. Only lightly scented, semi-double, bright orange-red flowers are produced from summer to autumn. Glossy foliage. Good in containers or as a hedge.
75 × 60cm/2½ × 2ft.

'Doris Tysterman' (1975) Large-flowered or hybrid tea. Fragrant, fully double, coppery orange flowers appear from summer to autumn. Good for bedding.
1.2 × 0.75m/4 × 2½ft.

'Ena Harkness' (1946) Large-flowered or hybrid tea. Fragrant, fully double, deep red flowers are produced from early summer to autumn.
75 × 60cm/2½ × 2ft.

'English Miss' (1978) Cluster-flowered or floribunda. Fragrant, fully double, camellia-like, soft blush-pink flowers appear from summer to autumn. Good in containers.
75 × 60cm/2½ × 2ft.

'Ernest H. Morse' (syn. 'E.H. Morse'; 1965) Large-flowered or hybrid tea. Very fragrant, double, red flowers, which darken with age, are borne freely from summer to autumn.
75 × 60cm/2½ × 2ft.

'Doris Tysterman'

'Evelyn Fison' (syn. 'Macev', 'Irish Wonder'; 1962) Cluster-flowered or floribunda. Virtually scentless, double, brilliant red flowers are produced from summer to autumn. Glossy foliage. Good for bedding.
70 × 60cm/28 × 24in.

'Fairyland' (syn. 'Harlayalong') Polyantha. Sweetly scented, cupped, fully double, rosette-shaped, soft-pink flowers are borne in trusses from summer to autumn. Glossy foliage.
0.6 × 1.2m/2 × 4ft.

'Fellowship' (syn. 'Harwelcome,' 'Livin' Easy'; 1992). Cluster-flowered or floribunda. Fragrant, double, cupped, warm-orange flowers appear from summer to autumn.
75 × 60cm/2½ × 2ft.

'Fragrant Delight' (1978) Cluster-flowered or floribunda. Fragrant, double, orange-tinged, salmon-pink flowers are produced from summer to autumn. Reddish-green foliage.
1 × 0.75m/3 × 2½ft.

'Fragrant Hour' Large-flowered or hybrid tea. Shapely, fragrant, salmon-pink flowers are produced in summer-autumn. Good for cutting.
1 × 1m/3 × 3ft.

'Freedom' (syn. 'Dicjem'; 1984) Large-flowered or hybrid tea. Only lightly scented, double, vivid yellow flowers are produced from summer to autumn. Good for bedding. Glossy mid-green foliage.
75 × 60cm/2½ × 2ft.

'Gertrude Jekyll' (syn. 'Ausbord'; 1986) Shrub. Large, very fragrant, fully double, deep pink flowers are borne from summer to autumn. Greyish-green foliage.
1.5 × 1m/5 × 3ft.

'Glenfiddich' (1976) Cluster-flowered or floribunda. Fragrant, double, golden-yellow flowers appear from summer to autumn. Glossy foliage.
75 × 60cm/2½ × 2ft.

'Golden Wings' (1956) Shrub. Lightly scented, single, pale golden-yellow flowers are produced throughout summer. Spreading habit.
1 × 1.2m/3 × 4ft.

'Simba'

'Harry Wheatcroft' Large-flowered or hybrid tea. Fragrant red flowers, borne in summer-autumn, are striped with rich golden yellow.
1 × 1m/3ft × 3ft.

'Heritage' (syn. 'Ausblush'; 1984) Shrub. Strongly scented, fully double, apricot-pink flowers are produced from summer to autumn.
1.2 × 1.2m/4 × 4ft.

'Iced Ginger' (1971) Cluster-flowered or floribunda. Only lightly scented, double, coppery pink flowers are borne from summer to autumn. Good for cutting.
1 × 0.75m/3 × 2½ft.

'Josephine Bruce' (1952) Large-flowered or hybrid tea. Very fragrant, shapely, double, rich deep crimson flowers are produced from summer to autumn. Makes a good standard.
75 × 60cm/2½ × 2ft.

'Keepsake' (syn. 'Kormalda', 'Esmeralda'; 1980) Large-flowered or hybrid tea. Fragrant, rain-resistant, fully double, warm pink flowers are are borne from summer to autumn.
75 × 60cm/2½ × 2ft.

'Lovely Lady' (syn. 'Dicjubell', 'Dickson's Jubilee'; 1986) Large-flowered or hybrid tea. Fragrant, fully double, warm-pink flowers appear from summer to autumn.
80 × 70cm/32 × 28in.

'Lovers' Meeting' (1980) Large-flowered or hybrid tea. Slightly fragrant, double, warm pinkish-orange flowers are produced from summer to autumn. Makes a good standard. Bronze-tinged foliage.
75 × 75cm/2½ × 2½ft.

'Marguerite Hilling' (syn. 'Pink Nevada'; 1959) Shrub. Lightly scented, semi-double, pale pink flowers appear in mid-summer and again, spasmodically, in autumn.
1.8 × 2.4m/6 × 8ft.

'Matangi' (syn. 'Macman'; 1974) Cluster-flowered or floribunda. Only lightly scented, double, brilliant vermilion flowers with white eyes and petal reverses are borne from summer to autumn. Glossy foliage.
80 × 60cm/32 × 24in.

'Mischief' (syn. 'Macmi'; 1961) Large-flowered or hybrid tea. Only lightly scented, double, deep salmon-pink flowers are borne from summer to autumn. Prone to rust.
1 × 0.6m/3 × 2ft.

'National Trust' (syn. 'Bad Nauheim'; 1970) Large-flowered or hybrid tea. Virtually scentless, fully double, vivid red flowers are produced from summer to autumn.
60 × 60cm/2 × 2ft.

'Piccolo' (syn. 'Piccola', 'Tanolokip'; 1984) Cluster-flowered or floribunda. Virtually scentless, double, vivid red flowers, which are rain-resistant, are produced from summer to autumn.
50 × 50cm/20 × 20in.

'Pot o' Gold' (syn. 'Dicdivine'; 1980) Large-flowered or hybrid tea. Dainty, fragrant, fully double, golden-yellow flowers are borne from summer to autumn. Makes a good standard.
75 × 60cm/2½ × 2ft.

'Precious Platinum' (syn. 'Opa Pötschke'; 1974) Large-flowered or hybrid tea. Only lightly scented, fully double, luminous red flowers are produced from summer to autumn.
1 × 0.6m/3 × 2ft.

'Prima Ballerina' (syn. 'Première Ballerina'; 1957) Large-flowered or hybrid tea. Sweetly scented, double, warm-pink flowers are borne from summer to autumn. Leathery foliage.
1 × 0.6m/3 × 2ft.

'Princess Michael of Kent' (syn. 'Harlightly'; 1981) Cluster-flowered or floribunda. Sweetly scented, fully double, clear-yellow flowers are produced from summer to autumn. Glossy foliage. Good in containers.
60 × 50cm/24 × 20in.

'Remember Me' (syn. 'Cocdestin'; 1984) Large-flowered or hybrid tea. Only lightly scented, fully double, warm coppery orange flowers are borne from summer to autumn. Glossy, dark green foliage.
1 × 0.6m/3 × 2ft.

'Rose Gaujard' (syn. 'Gaumo'; 1957) Large-flowered or hybrid tea. Fragrant, fully double, cherry red flowers with pale pink petal reverses are produced from summer to autumn. Good for cutting.
1 × 0.75m/3 × 2½ft.

'Rosemary Harkness' (syn. 'Harrowbond'; 1985) Large-flowered or hybrid tea. Fragrant, double, orange-yellow to salmon-pink flowers appear from summer to autumn. Glossy foliage. Good for cutting.
80 × 80cm/32 × 32in.

'Royal Highness' (syn. 'Königliche Hoheit'; 1962) Large-flowered or hybrid tea. Strongly fragrant, shapely, fully double, blush pink flowers are borne from summer to autumn.
1 × 0.6m/3 × 2ft.

'Ruby Wedding' Large-flowered or hybrid tea. Double, scented, deep velvety-red flowers are produced in succession throughout summer and autumn. Glossy leaves.
75 × 75cm/2½ × 2½ft.

'Silver Jubilee' (1978) Large-flowered or hybrid tea. Lightly scented, fully double, soft-pink flowers shaded with apricot-pink are borne freely from summer to autumn.
1 × 0.75m/3 × 2½ft.

'Simba' (syn. 'Goldsmith', 'Helmut Schmidt', 'Korbelma'; 1981) Large-flowered or hybrid tea. Scented, double, clear-yellow, rain-resistant flowers are produced from summer to autumn. Good for cutting.
75 × 60cm/2½ × 2ft.

'Tango' (syn. 'Macfirwal', 'Rock 'n' Roll', 'Stretch Johnson'; 1988) Cluster-flowered or floribunda. Lightly scented, semi-double flowers, the petals, fimbriated (frilled) at the edges, are orange-red with white rims, yellow at the base and on the reverse, and are borne in summer to autumn. Good for bedding.
75 × 60cm/2½ × 2ft.

'The Lady'

'Tequila Sunrise' (syn. 'Dicobey', 'Beaulieu'; 1989) Large-flowered or hybrid tea. Only lightly scented, double, vivid yellow flowers with scarlet petal edges appear from summer to autumn.
75 × 60cm/2½ × 2ft.

'The Lady' (syn. 'Fryjingo'; 1985) Shrub. Fragrant, double, yellow flowers, flushed salmon-pink and rain-resistant, are produced from summer to autumn.
1 × 0.6m/3 × 2ft.

'Valencia' (syn. 'Koreklia'; 1989) Large-flowered or hybrid tea. Fragrant, double, warm golden-yellow flowers are carried from summer to autumn. Tolerates light shade. Leathery, glossy foliage.
1 × 0.6m/3 × 2ft.

'Warm Wishes' (syn. 'Fryxotic'; 1994) Large-flowered or hybrid tea. Sweetly scented, double, warm salmon-pink flowers are borne from summer to autumn. Glossy foliage. Good for cutting.
1 × 0.75m/3 × 2½ft.

Other recommended climbing roses

'Alister Stella Gray' (syn. 'Golden Rambler'; 1894) Climbing noisette. Clusters of very fragrant, fully double, quartered-rosette, deep yellow flowers are borne from summer to autumn. Vigorous upright stems with mid-green, glossy foliage. Suitable for growing into a tree.
5 × 3m/16½ × 10ft.

'Altissimo' (syn. 'Delmur'; 1966) Climber. Single, cupped, vivid red flowers, with golden stamens, are produced from summer to autumn. A stiffly upright plant.
3 × 2.4m/10 × 8ft.

'Bad Neuenahr' Climbing rose with large, double, clear-red flowers borne in summer and autumn.
3 × 1.5m/10ft × 5ft.

'Bantry Bay' (1967) Climbing large-flowered or climbing hybrid tea. Large, freely borne clusters of lightly scented, cupped, semi-double, clear-pink flowers open flat from summer to autumn. Glossy foliage.
4 × 2.4m/13 × 8ft.

'Belle Portugaise' (syn. 'Belle of Portugal') Climbing tea. Sweetly scented, pointed, double, salmon-pink flowers are carried in summer. Large, glossy leaves. A vigorous plant.
6 × 3m/20ft × 10ft.

'Blush Rambler' (1903) Rambler. Clusters of sweetly scented, cupped, semi-double, pale pink flowers are borne in mid- to late summer. The glossy foliage is abundant and mid-green in colour. This rose is suitable for growing into a tree or over a pergola. It has a spreading habit.
4 × 5m/13 × 16½ft.

'Bantry Bay'

'Blush Rambler'

'Céline Forestier' (1842) Climbing noisette. Fragrant, rounded, double, quartered, creamy yellow flowers appear from late spring to autumn. Requires some protection in winter.
2.4 × 1.2m/8 × 4ft.

'City Girl' (syn. 'Harzorba'; 1994) Climber. Fragrant, semi-double, creamy pink flowers are carried from summer to autumn. Glossy, dark green foliage.
2.4 × 2.4m/8 × 8ft.

'Climbing Etoile de Hollande' (1931) Climbing large-flowered or climbing hybrid tea. Fragrant, cupped, double, deep red flowers appear throughout summer.
6 × 5m/20 × 16½ft.

'Climbing Lady Hillingdon' (1917) Climbing tea. Sweetly scented, double, apricot-yellow flowers open from pointed buds from summer to autumn. Requires the protection of a west- or south-facing wall. Dark green foliage with reddish stems.
5 × 2.4m/16½ × 8ft.

'Climbing Masquerade' (1958) Climbing cluster-flowered or climbing floribunda. Clusters of semi-double flowers, which open yellow, then change to pink and age to red, are borne from summer to autumn, with all colours appearing on the plant simultaneously.
2.4 × 1.5m/8 × 5ft.

'Climbing Mrs Sam McGredy' (1937) Climbing large-flowered or

climbing hybrid tea. Fragrant, fully double, coppery red flowers are borne in mid-summer and again, but sporadically, in autumn. A stiffly upright plant. Foliage is glossy and reddish-green in colour.
3 × 3m/10 × 10ft.

'Climbing Shot Silk' (1931) Climbing large-flowered or climbing hybrid tea. Heavily fragrant, fully double, urn-shaped to cupped flowers of pink overlaid with yellow and orange, are produced in summer. Glossy dark green foliage.
3 × 2.4m/10 × 8ft.

'Copenhagen' (1964) Climbing large-flowered or climbing hybrid tea. Fragrant, double, scarlet flowers are carried in summer and autumn.
3 × 1.5m/10 × 5ft.

'Crimson Shower' (1951) Rambler. Clusters of double, rosette-shaped, bright red flowers are produced from summer to autumn. Glossy foliage.
2.4 × 2.1m/8 × 7ft.

'Dorothy Perkins' (1901) Rambler. Clusters of scentless, double, bright pink flowers appear from late summer to autumn.
3 × 3m/10 × 10ft.

'Don Juan' Climbing rose with a succession of large, fragrant, deep red flowers throughout summer.
3 × 1.5m/10 × 5ft.

'Climbing Shot Silk'

'Dreaming Spires' (1973) Climber. Large, pleasantly scented, double, rounded, rich yellow flowers are produced from summer to autumn. Foliage is glossy and dark green. This rose has a stiffly upright habit.
3 × 2.1m/10 × 7ft.

'Easlea's Golden Rambler' (syn. 'Easlea's Golden'; 1932) Rambler. Clusters of fragrant, fully double, rounded, apricot-yellow flowers, marked with red, appear in summer.
6 × 5m/20 × 16½ft.

'Emily Gray' (1918) Rambler. Clusters of sweetly scented, double, rounded, buff-yellow flowers are borne from early summer. Glossy, almost evergreen foliage. Often prone to mildew.
5 × 3m/16½ × 10ft.

'Excelsa' (syn. 'Red Dorothy Perkins'; 1909) Rambler. Clusters of rosette-shaped, double, red flowers are produced in summer. Glossy dark green foliage. Lax habit. A suitable rose for growing into a tree or up a pillar.
4 × 3m/13 × 10ft.

'Félicité Perpétue' (syn. 'Climbing Little White Pet', 'Félicité et Perpétue'; 1827) Rambler. Fragrant, fully double, rosette-shaped, light pink to ivory white flowers are produced in summer. Almost evergreen in favourable conditions. This rose will tolerate some shade.
5 × 4m/16½ × 13ft.

***filipes* 'Kiftsgate'** Climbing rose. Clusters of single, flat, creamy white flowers are borne in late summer. Abundant, light green, glossy foliage. A very vigorous rose which works well grown into a tree.
10 × 10m/30 × 30ft.

'Dreaming Spires'

'François Juranville' (1906) Rambler. Fragrant, fully double, rosette-shaped, pale salmon-pink flowers are produced in summer. There is abundant glossy foliage. Prone to mildew in a dry site, particularly when grown against a wall.
6 × 5m/20 × 16½ft.
'Galway Bay' (syn. 'Macba'; 1966) Climbing large-flowered or climbing hybrid tea. Large, double, rich pink flowers are borne from summer to autumn.
3 × 1.8m/10 × 6ft.
'Goldfinch' (1907) Rambler. Scented, double, rosette-shaped, deep yellow flowers, fading to pale cream, are produced in summer. Comparatively free of thorns with attractive light green foliage. Tolerates some shade.
2.4 × 1.8m/8 × 6ft.
'Guinée' (1938) Climbing large-flowered or climbing hybrid tea. Very fragrant, fully double, cupped, rich dark red flowers are borne in summer. Dark stems and foliage. Prone to mildew.
5 × 2.1m/16½ × 7ft.
'Hamburger Phönix' (1954) Rambler. Slightly fragrant, semi-double, deep red flowers open flat in summer and autumn.
3 × 1.5m/10 × 5ft.

'Excelsa'

'High Hopes' (syn. 'Haryup'; 1992) Climber. Fragrant, double, light pink flowers are borne from summer to autumn. Glossy foliage.
4 × 2.4m/13 × 8ft.
'Leaping Salmon' (syn. 'Peamight'; 1986) Climbing large-flowered or climbing hybrid tea. Sweetly scented, double, urn-shaped, salmon-pink flowers are borne in summer and autumn.
3 × 1.8m/10 × 6ft.
'Leverkusen' (1954) Climber. Clusters of fragrant, double, light yellow flowers are produced from summer to autumn. Glossy, dark green foliage.
3 × 2.1m/10 × 7ft.
'Meg' (1954) Climbing large-flowered or climbing hybrid tea. Clusters of fragrant, large, semi-double, warm buff, apricot and peach-pink flowers open flat from summer to autumn. Dark foliage.
4 × 4m/13 × 13ft.
mulliganii (syn. *R. longicuspis*; 1919) Rambling species. Large clusters of delicately scented, single, white flowers are borne in summer. Suitable for growing into a tree.
6 × 3m/20 × 10ft.
'New Dawn' (syn. 'The New Dawn', 'Everblooming Dr W. van Fleet'; 1930) Climber. Clusters of fragrant, fully double, cupped, sweetly scented shell-pink flowers, which fade to white as they age, are produced over a long period from summer to autumn. Striking, glossy foliage. Hardy enough to tolerate a north-facing wall.
3 × 2.4m/10 × 8ft.
'Night Light' (syn. 'Poullight'; 1982) Climber. Fragrant, double, rounded,

'New Dawn'

yellow flowers are produced from summer to autumn.
2.4 × 2.1m/8 × 7ft.
'Niphetos' Climbing tea rose. Round, double white flowers are borne in summer with a second, less abundant, flush in autumn. Light green, pointed leaves.
3 × 2m/10 × 6½ft.
'Paul's Himalayan Musk' (syn. 'Paul's Himalayan Rambler'; 'Paul's Himalayan Musk Rambler'; 1916) Rambler. Clusters of fragrant, double, rosette-shaped, pale pink flowers are borne in summer. A thorny rose.
10 × 10m/33 × 33ft.
'Paul's Scarlet Climber' (1916) Climber. Clusters of virtually scentless, cupped, double, bright red flowers, which gradually age to purplish-grey, are borne in summer. It will tolerate some shade.
3 × 3m/10 × 10ft.
'Penny Lane' (syn. 'Hardwell') Climbing rose with a succession of fragrant, honey-coloured flowers all summer.
4 × 1.8m/13 × 6ft
'Ramona' (syn. *R.* × *amenoides* 'Ramonda', 'Red Cherokee'; 1913) Climber. Virtually scentless, single, intense red flowers open flat to reveal golden stamens in early summer.
2.4 × 3m/8 × 10ft.
'Ritter von Barmstede' (1960) Climber. Large clusters of fragrant, small, double, deep pink flowers are produced in summer and autumn.
3 × 1.5m/10 × 5ft.
'Rosy Mantle' (1968) Climber. Slightly fragrant, fully double, deep pink flowers are borne from summer to autumn. Foliage is dark green and rather sparse.
2.4 × 1.8m/8 × 6ft.
'Royal Gold' (1957) Climbing large-flowered or climbing hybrid tea. Slightly fragrant, double, deep yellow flowers are produced in summer and again in autumn. Slightly tender.
2.4 × 1.2m/8 × 4ft.
'Sander's White Rambler' Rambler. Clusters of fragrant, fully double, deep, rosette, white flowers are produced in late summer.
3 × 2.4m/10 × 8ft.
'Sophie's Perpetual' (syn. 'Dresden China') Climbing China. Clusters of well-scented, almost globular, semi-double, blush pink flowers, overlaid with deep pink and cerise, are borne continuously from summer to autumn.
2.4 × 1.2m/8 × 4ft.
'Souvenir de Claudius Denoyel' (1920) Award-winning climbing large-flowered or climbing hybrid tea. Fragrant, cupped, bright

'Paul's Himalayan Musk'

crimson flowers are produced in mid-summer, with a second, later flush in autumn.
5 × 3m/16½ × 10ft.
'Swan Lake' (1968) Climber. Slightly fragrant, double, urn-shaped, ivory white flowers, tinged pink, are borne in summer. There is some repeat flowering.
3 × 1.8m/10 × 6ft.
'The Garland' (1835) Rambler. Clusters of small, fragrant, semi-double, blush pink flowers, which fade to white, are borne in summer.
5 × 3m/16½ × 10ft.
'Wedding Day' (1951) Rambler. Large clusters of fragrant, single, creamy yellow flowers, which quickly fade to pale pink, are produced in summer. A vigorous variety, good for growing into a tree.
8 × 4m/26 × 13ft.

Other recommended miniature roses

'Arizona Sunset' Miniature. Clusters of small, cupped, pale yellow flowers, flushed with orange-red, are borne throughout summer and autumn. Good for cutting.
40 × 30cm/16 × 12in.

'Baby Masquerade' (syn. 'Tanba', 'Baby Carnival'; 1966) Miniature. Clusters of many small, double, rosette-shaped, yellow flowers, flushed with pink and red, are borne freely over a long period from summer to autumn. It has dense, leathery foliage. Usually looks better planted in groups rather than as an individual plant. A good rose for low edging.
40 × 40cm/16 × 16in.

'Bit o' Sunshine' Miniature. Masses of small, double, rather flat, pale yellow flowers are produced from summer to autumn. A reliable plant. Ideal for containers of all types and for border edging.
30 × 30cm/12 × 12in.

'Bonica' (syn. 'Bonica '82', 'Meidonomac') Award-winning ground-cover rose. Large clusters of lightly scented, double, clear-pink flowers are produced freely from summer to autumn. Abundant glossy foliage. A good rose for beds, borders and low hedges.
1 × 1m/3 × 3ft.

'Baby Masquerade'

'Bit o' Sunshine'

'Chatsworth' (syn. 'Mirato', 'Tanotari', 'Tanotax') Dwarf cluster-flowered or patio rose. Broad clusters of many small, double, cupped, deep rich pink flowers are borne from summer to autumn.
0.6 × 1m/2 × 3ft.

'Climbing Pompon de Paris' Miniature climber. Many small, double, rich red, rather button-like flowers are borne in early summer. The foliage is grey-green with flexible stems which can be easily trained against a wall.
3.5 × 2.4m/11 × 8ft.

'Colibre '79' (syn. 'Colibre '80'; 'Colibri '79', 'Medianover') Miniature. Clusters of urn-shaped, cupped, double flowers of unusual colouring: the orange-yellow ground colour is heavily veined with deep red-pink. Flowers are produced freely from summer to autumn. An upright plant, ideal for window boxes or small containers.
30 × 30cm/12 × 12in.

'Dresden Doll' Miniature moss. Scented, fully double, cupped flowers, which are a beautiful shade of soft shell-pink, repeat well from summer to autumn. Ideal for window boxes and troughs.
25 × 15cm/20 × 6in.

'Easter Morning' (syn. 'Easter Morn') Miniature. Lightly scented, double, urn shaped creamy white flowers are borne freely from summer to autumn. Glossy dark green foliage.
40 × 25cm/16 × 10in.

'Essex' (syn. 'Poulnoz', 'Pink Cover') Ground-cover rose. Sprays of small, single, star-like, rich pink flowers with white centres are borne on long

stems throughout summer and into autumn. Dark, glossy foliage.
0.6 × 1.2m/2 × 4ft.

'Ferdy' (syn. 'Ferdi', 'Keitoli'; 1984) Ground-cover rose. Dense clusters of only lightly scented, small, double, bright pink flowers are borne from summer to autumn.
0.75 × 1.2m/2½ × 4ft.

'Fire Princess' Miniature. Sprays of small, fully double rosette-shaped, vibrant orange-red flowers provide a vivid contrast against the small, dark, glossy leaves from summer to autumn. Upright habit.
45 × 40cm/18 × 16in.

'Gentle Touch' (syn. 'Diclulu'; 1986) Award-winning dwarf cluster-flowered or patio rose. Clusters of lightly scented, perfectly urn-shaped, semi-double flowers of the softest pale pink are borne in profusion from summer to autumn. Dark, glossy foliage. Good for low hedges or border edging. A strong and sturdy plant.
40 × 40cm/16 × 16in.

'Gingernut' (syn. 'Coccrazy') Dwarf cluster-flowered or patio rose. Dense clusters of cupped flowers with unusual colouring – orange-bronze, overlaid with red and pink – are borne from summer to autumn. Suitable for low edging.
40 × 45cm/16 × 18in.

'Good as Gold' (syn. 'Chewsunbeam'; 1995) Miniature climber. Clusters of pleasantly scented, double, rich yellow flowers with pointed petals, which open from urn-shaped buds in almost continuous succession, are produced from summer to autumn.
1.8 × 1.5m/6 × 5ft.

'Colibre '79'

'Grouse'

'Bonica'

'Grouse' (syn. 'Immensee', 'Korimro', 'Lac Rose'; 1984) Ground-cover rose. Fragrant, small, single, flat, blush-pink flowers, with a boss of golden stamens, are borne in summer. The foliage is dark, glossy and abundant. Good for covering a bank or as a weeping standard.
0.6 × 3m/2 × 10ft.

'Hertfordshire' (syn. 'Kortenay', 'Tommeliese'; 1991) Ground-cover rose. Many, fragrant, single, vivid pink flowers with a boss of golden stamens are produced over a very long flowering period from summer to autumn.
0.45 × 1m/1½ × 3ft.

'Hotline' (syn. 'Aromikeh') Miniature. High-pointed, semi-double red flowers are produced from summer to autumn.
45 × 35cm/18 × 14in.

'Little Flirt'

'**Hula Girl**' (1975) Miniature. Slightly scented, fully double, urn-shaped, salmon-orange flowers are produced freely from summer to autumn. Dark green, glossy foliage.
45 × 40cm/18 × 16in.

'**Jeanne Lajoie**' Miniature climber. Fully double, high-pointed, soft lavender-pink flowers are borne from summer to autumn. Dark, glossy foliage.
1.8 × 0.75m/6 × 2½ft.

'**Laura Ashley**' (syn. 'Chewharia') Ground-cover rose. Profuse clusters of many sweetly scented, small, single, slightly cupped, magenta to lilac-pink flowers are produced freely from summer to autumn.
0.6 × 1.2m/2 × 4ft.

'**Little Bo-peep**' (syn. 'Poullen'; 1992) Dwarf cluster-flowered or patio rose. Dense clusters of small, semi-double, rather flattened, pale pink flowers are produced from summer to autumn.
30 × 50cm/12 × 20in.

'Partridge'

'**Little Flirt**' Miniature. Small, double blooms open from buds of brilliant pink, with a paler pink petal reverse, the colour fading quickly in strong sunlight. Ideal for window boxes and containers.
40 × 25cm/16 × 10in.

'**Little Rambler**' (syn. 'Chewramb'; 1994) Miniature rambler. Clusters of small, fully double, rosette-shaped, soft-pink flowers are produced from summer to autumn, a long period for a rambler.
2.1 × 2.1m/7 × 7ft.

'**Magic Carousel**' (syn. 'Moorcar') Miniature. Small, lightly scented rosette-shaped, pale yellow flowers with crimson petal margins are produced from summer to autumn. Small, glossy leaves. Suitable for a window box or as a low edging.
40 × 30cm/16 × 12in.

'**Nozomi**' (syn. 'Heideröslein'; 1968) Miniature climber. Many small, single, flat, starry soft blush-pink flowers are borne in summer, occasionally with a second flush of blooms in late summer. A good container plant.
0.45 × 1.2m/1½ × 4ft.

'**Partridge**' (syn. 'Korweirim', 'Lac Blanc', 'Weisse Immensee') Ground-cover rose. Small, glossy, dark green leaves are almost obscured in mid-summer by sprays of sweetly scented, small, single, slightly cupped, white flowers.
0.6 × 3m/2 × 10ft.

'**Party Girl**' Miniature. Fragrant, beautifully formed, high-centred,

'Pink Chimo'

'Pink Meidiland'

apricot-yellow flowers, flushed with salmon-pink, are borne from summer to autumn. Can be grown as a houseplant in good light.
35 × 35cm/14 × 14in.

'Pheasant' (syn. 'Heidekönigin', 'Kordapt') Ground-cover rose. Long stems are wreathed in cupped, double, pale pink flowers, with golden stamens, in mid-summer only.
0.45 × 3m/1½ × 10ft.

'Pink Bells' (syn. 'Poulbells'; 1983) Ground-cover rose. Long stems bear many clusters of small, double, bright pink pompon blooms, once only in mid-summer. Small, dark green leaves.
1 × 1.2m/3 × 4ft or more.

'Pink Chimo' (syn. 'Interchimp') Ground-cover shrub. Cupped, semi-double, deep pink flowers wreath the stems from summer to autumn.
0.6 × 1m/2 × 3ft.

'Pink Meidiland' (syn. 'Meipoque') Ground-cover rose. Attractive, relatively large, single, cupped, bright carmine-pink flowers with white centres and golden stamens are borne in clusters from summer to autumn. Good for a low hedge.
1 × 0.75m/3 × 2½ft.

'Red Blanket' (syn. 'Intercell') Ground-cover shrub. Clusters of well-formed, flat, semi-double flowers, pale pink at the centre shading to red-pink at the margins, appear from summer to autumn.
0.75 × 1.2m/2½ × 4ft.

'Snow Carpet' (syn. 'Maccarpe'; 1980) Ground-cover rose. Fully double, creamy white, pompon flowers are produced over a long period in mid-summer. Leaves are small but glossy and plentiful.
15 × 45cm/6 × 18in.

'Stacey Sue'

'Snowball' (syn. 'Angelita'; 'Macangeli') Miniature. Small, pompon, fully double white flowers are borne from summer to autumn. Abundant small, glossy leaves.
20 × 30cm/8 × 12in.

'Stacey Sue' (1976) Miniature. Well-filled pretty sprays of small, rosette-shaped, pink flowers are borne from summer to autumn amongst neat, glossy dark green foliage. A well-proportioned miniature.
25 × 30cm/10 × 12in.

'Starina' (syn. 'Meigabi'; 1965) Miniature. Scentless, double, vivid vermilion-orange flowers are borne from summer to autumn.
45 × 35cm/18 × 14in.

'Suma' (syn. 'Harsuma'; 1989) Ground-cover rose. Virtually scentless, fully double, deep pink flowers, sometimes with white margins, are borne from summer to autumn.
0.6 × 1.5m/2 × 5ft.

'The Valois Rose' (syn. 'Kordadel') Miniature. Clusters of lightly scented, creamy-yellow, rounded flowers, shaded with carmine at the petal margins, are produced from summer to autumn. Perfect in containers or as low edging at the front of a border.
40 × 30cm/16 × 12in.

Glossary

Anther The part of the STAMEN that is carried at the top of the FILAMENT and bears the POLLEN.

Axil The angle between a part of a plant, such as a leaf stalk, and the stem on which it is borne.

Bare-rooted Of plants, having been lifted from the ground while dormant and the roots shaken free of soil before being sold.

Biennial A plant that is sown one year to flower and fruit the next, dying in the second season after germination.

Binomial A name with two parts, that of the GENUS – for example, Rosa – and, usually, that of the SPECIES – for example, *gallica* – which distinguishes a group of plants from other groups within the same genus.

Blind Of a plant, one that does not flower because the growing point has been damaged.

Bract A modified leaf or leaf-like structure, arising from a flower stem, that appears to form part of a flower-head.

Budding The means by which nearly all roses are propagated commercially. The growth bud of a garden rose is inserted into the rootstock of a species rose.

Calyx (pl. calyces) The group of modified leaves that enclose a flower bud.

Cambium The living tissue immediately beneath the bark of a stem or branch.

Cane The hollow or straight stem of a plant, used to support climbing roses.

Catenary The curve created by a flexible cord supported between two points.

Chlorosis The loss of green coloration in leaves; it may be due to a mineral deficiency, lack of light or disease.

Climber Of a plant, one that ascends, using another plant or an object for support by means of modified roots, leaves (tendrils) or leaf stalks. A plant that needs to be tied to its support is a trailer, rather than a true climber.

Cluster A group of flowers, leaves and so on that arise, or appear to arise, from a single point.

Cultivar A word, derived from *culti*vated *var*iety and abbreviated to cv., that is applied to a plant that was developed and persisted in cultivation, as distinct from a SPECIES.

Cup-shaped Of a flower, hemispherical with straight or slightly spreading sides.

Cutting That part of a root, leaf or stem that is taken from a parent plant and used for propagation.

Deadhead To remove dead flower-heads from plants in order to encourage the production of further flowers by preventing the development of seed heads.

Deciduous Of plants, shedding leaves in winter. See also EVERGREEN.

Disbudding The removal of side shoots and surplus shoots so that the plant's energies are concentrated on the remaining single bud. The practice is common among those who grow for exhibition or for cut flower arrangements.

Dormancy Of a plant, the period (usually winter) when it has temporarily stopped growing.

Double Of a flower, with more than the usual number of petals – that is, the number seen on the normal wild plant. See also SEMI-DOUBLE; SINGLE.

Evergreen Of plants, retaining leaves in a functional form for more than one growing season. See also DECIDUOUS.

Family The category in plant classification that lies between order and genus. A group of genera forms a family. Roses belong to the Rosaceae family.

Filament A fine, thread-like stem that carries the ANTHER in a STAMEN.

Fimbriated Of flowers, having petals that are divided or fringed at the edges.

Foliar feed A fertilizer that is applied to a plant's leaves, usually by means of a fine, dilute spray.

Genus The category in plant classification that lies between family and species, and the smallest naturally occurring group to contain distinct but related species. Roses are members of the genus *Rosa*.

Grafting A method of propagation by which a stem or bud of one plant is joined to the root of another so that they form a new plant.

Half-standard Of a tree that has an unbranched trunk to about 1.2m/4ft from ground level.

Hardwood cutting A cutting taken from mature wood after leaf fall – that is, from early autumn to early winter. Such cuttings often take longer to root than SOFTWOOD CUTTINGS.

Hip The fruit of the rose. Some rose varieties are grown for their ornamental red hips.

Humus Decayed vegetable matter found in the soil. Humus may also be garden compost or leaf mould. The activity of bacteria in breaking down organic matter releases the chemicals in a form that plants are able to absorb as nutrients.

Hybrid A plant that arises as the result of the cross-fertilization of two or more species or genera.

Lateral A shoot or stem branching off from the main stem, especially from a leaf AXIL of the main stem.

Layering A method of propagation in which a shoot is encouraged to form roots while it is still attached to the parent plant.

Leaf cutter A type of bee which uses powerful jaws to shear off oval portions of leaves, which are used for her eggs.

Loam Fertile, well-drained soil that contains neither too much sand nor too much clay and is rich in HUMUS.

Mulch A top-dressing, usually of organic material, applied to the soil around plants to keep down weeds and conserve moisture. It may provide some nutrients.

Mutation An accidental variation from an original, often called a sport.

Pedicel The solitary stalk of a single flower in a CLUSTER.

Peduncle The stalk of a single flower or the main stalk of a CLUSTER of flowers.

Perennial A plant that lives for more than two years, normally flowering each year. Perennials usually die down in winter, with new growth appearing in the spring.

Pollen The male fertilizing powder formed in the ANTHERS.

Prostrate Of a plant, with its trailing stems lying flat along the ground.

Remontant Of a plant, one that flowers in flushes through a season.

Rootstock The plant on which another is grafted. See also GRAFTING; SUCKER.

Rosette-shaped Of a flower, having petals that radiate from a single point.

Selective weedkiller Although harmless to nearby plants, a hormone weedkiller that affects the growth of selected plants.

Semi-double Of a flower, with just a few more petals than is usual. See also DOUBLE; SINGLE.

Sepal Part of the CALYX protecting the flower bud.

Single Of a flower, with the normal number of petals for the species arranged in a single whorl. A single rose has five petals.

Softwood cutting A cutting taking from young, non-woody growth during the growing season – that is, from spring to early summer.

Species The taxonomic rank below genus. The name is given to a group of plants that will interbreed but will not normally breed with members of another group.

Sport A plant that varies spontaneously from the usual, either in flower or leaf form. A mutation, which may be induced or which may arise accidentally.

Stamen The POLLEN-producing part of a flower consisting, usually, of ANTHER and FILAMENT.

Sucker A shoot that arises from the base of a parent plant, often directly from the root, rather than from the stem or crown.

Index

Acknowledgements

This edition is published by Lorenz Books
an imprint of Anness Publishing Ltd
www.lorenzbooks.com
www.annesspublishing.com

If you like the images in this book and would like to investigate using them for publishing, promotions or advertising, please visit our website www.practicalpictures.com for more information.

© Anness Publishing Ltd 2022

All rights reserved. No part of this publication may be reproduced, stored in a retrieval system, or transmitted in any way or by any means, electronic, mechanical, photocopying, recording or otherwise, without the prior written permission of the copyright holder.

A CIP catalogue record for this book is available from the British Library.

Publisher: Joanna Lorenz
Senior Editor: Felicity Forster
Author of Miniature Roses section: Lin Hawthorne
Designer: Lilian Lindblom
Production Controller: Ben Worley

PUBLISHER'S NOTE
Although the advice and information in this book are believed to be accurate at the time of going to press, neither the authors nor the publisher can accept any legal responsibility or liability for any errors or omissions that may have been made nor for any inaccuracies nor for any loss, harm or injury that comes about from following instructions or advice in this book.

The publisher would like to thank the following for their help in the production of this book: Ann Hartley, Long Buckby, Northants; Cants of Colchester, Colchester; Cottesbrooke Hall Gardens, Cottesbrooke, Northants; Gandy's Roses Ltd, North Kilworth, Leics; Haddonstone Ltd, East Haddon, North Hants; J. F. Arbuthnott, Stone, Worcs; Janine Hurry, Long Buckby; Northants; Mattock's Roses, Nuneham Courtenay, Oxon; Mr and Mrs A. Keech, Long Buckby, Northants; Mr and Mrs A. Shepherd, Long Buckby, Northants; Mr and Mrs Smith, Nobottle, Northants; Ravensthorpe Nursery, Ravensthorpe, Northants; Rearsby Roses, Rearsby, Leics; RHS Garden, Wisley; Royal National Rose Society, St Albans, Herts; Shirley Allen, Long Buckby, Northants; The Hon. Simon and Mrs Howard, Castle Howard, York.

All pictures were taken by Peter Anderson with the exception of the following (t=top, b=bottom, l=left, r=right, c=centre):
A–Z Botanical Collection: 154t.
Alamy: 24, 50.
The Harpur Garden Picture Library: 118–19 (Fudler's Hall, Chelmsford), 125l, 126l (Design: Tessa Hobbs), 127 (Stellenberg).
Harry Smith Collection: 155, 157, 160t.
John Freeman: 160b.
Marie O'Hara: 82–3, 86, 87t, 87b, 88, 89, 90t, 90b, 91, 92t, 95tl, 95tr, 95b, 96t, 96b, 97tl, 97b, 98tl, 98tr, 98b, 99b, 103tl, 103tr, 103b, 104tl, 104tr, 104b, 105t, 105b, 106tl, 106tr, 106b, 107t, 107b, 108tl, 108tr, 108b, 109t, 109b, 110t, 110bl, 110br, 111t, 111b, 112t, 112b, 113t, 113bl, 113br, 114b, 115t, 115bl, 115br, 186t, 186b, 187, 197 (all steps), 209, 217 (all steps), 222 (all steps), 223 (step 3, 4, 5 and 8), 231b, 238, 239, 240, 241.
Peter McHoy: 55, 58, 121, 125r, 242l, 243t, 243b.
Additional photography by Peter McHoy and John Freeman.